Family at Work

Family at Work explores how our family experience – its joys, challenges, and difficulties – affects how we take up our roles and how family dynamics can be re-enacted in the workplace.

Our family in the mind is the family we unconsciously project onto colleagues, bosses, and leaders, attributing characteristics and raising expectations from family roles we have experienced in our early life. Developing awareness and an understanding of what we project of our early experience in a work context can help to shift disruptive dynamics and allow us to be more ourselves, without feeling trapped in repeating family patterns. In this book, the author draws upon her extensive professional experience as an organisational coach and consultant to explore the impact such dynamics have on our working environment.

This is key reading for leaders, family business members, psychoanalysts, organizational consultants, psychologists, HR and business managers, and anyone who wants to understand how family dynamics affect the workplace.

Francesca Cardona is an organizational consultant, executive coach, and a teacher of consultancy. Italian by birth, she has been based in London since the mid-eighties. She has worked in a variety of organizational and cultural contexts, helping leaders, teams, and individuals to face issues of change, transition, and conflict and the emotional dimension of organizational life. She is the author of *Work Matters – Consulting to Leaders and Organizations in in the Tavistock Tradition* (2020).

'In this insightful and moving book, Francesca Cardona reveals the way our family experiences, past and present, real and imagined, infuse and inform our work. We do not just bring ourselves to the workplace, she reminds us. We also bring those who have had a role in shaping ourselves. And once you think of family that way, work becomes a place where we might repeat or change the ways of thinking, feeling, and behaving that make us who we are. It is a deeply human and very practical way of approaching work. Whether you see your work and family are intertwined, as in a family business, or you believe that they are separate, you will benefit – and enjoy – the cases, insights, and lessons in this book.'

Gianpiero Petriglieri, MD, *associate professor of organisational behaviour, INSEAD*

'Francesca Cardona masterfully illuminates the often invisible threads connecting our earliest family roles to our most pressing workplace challenges, showing us how the "unthought known" quietly shapes our professional identities, relationships, choices, and effectiveness. Through a psychodynamic lens, she transforms what might seem like ordinary workplace dynamics in both family and non-family businesses—rivalry with colleagues, difficulty with authority, fear of succession—into profound opportunities for self-understanding and growth. This book is essential reading for leaders and consultants seeking insight on how to be more fully present and effective in our professional lives and workplaces.'

Debbie Bing, *president, CFAR Consulting and Coaching, chair of the Family Firm Institute*

'We spend much of our adult lives at work. Yet how much do we consider the internal templates that we bring into the workplace – the "family in our mind" – which shapes how much work is a source of creativity and fulfilment or frustration and struggle. In this brilliantly engaging book, Francesca Cardona brings this to life for us. She draws deftly on psychoanalytic theory, using compelling stories from her experience as a consultant to organisations, to show us that such understanding may enable us to find our way toward new thinking and development, where previously we had been caught in frustrating repetition. I have always thought the psychoanalytic understanding of our organisational world, and how we function within this, is one that needs to reach a wider audience. Francesca Cardona speaks to all of us who spend much of our time in organisations – with this fascinating, and above all, supremely helpful book, which opens the door on how the private life of our internal worlds is expressed in the public realm of our working lives.'

Andrew Balfour PhD, CPsychol, *chief executive consultant, clinical psychologist, adult & couple psychotherapist*

Family at Work

How Family Dynamics Shape Our Working Lives

Francesca Cardona

Routledge
Taylor & Francis Group
LONDON AND NEW YORK

Designed cover image: © Luca Picardi

First published 2027
by Routledge
4 Park Square, Milton Park, Abingdon, Oxon OX14 4RN

and by Routledge
605 Third Avenue, New York, NY 10158

Routledge is an imprint of the Taylor & Francis Group, an informa business

British Library Cataloguing-in-Publication Data
A catalogue record for this book is available from the British Library

ISBN: 9781041012672 (hbk)
ISBN: 9781041004967 (pbk)
ISBN: 9781003613961 (ebk)

DOI: 10.4324/9781003613961

Typeset in Bembo
by codeMantra

To Maia, Leo, and Paris

Contents

Foreword

This is a fascinating book, drawing together past, present, and future with the individual, group, organization, and family in the mind. It is exceptionally easy to read and to grasp the underlying concepts. Because it is based on understanding how family dynamics influence our current roles, and because the majority of readers will have their own experiences of family dynamics in more or less dysfunctional form, it is easy to identify with the case studies presented and, in so doing, to begin to think about how our own family patterns have impacted on how we behave in the workplace and even on our choice of occupation.

I have known Francesca for several decades, and we have worked together in various settings, including in peer supervision, where I have found her comments on my own casework personally very helpful. She has developed a fabulous practice in coaching and organizational consultancy.

For this book, she uses the concept of Kintsugi – healing the cracks in ceramics with gold, thereby making them visible and the ceramic even more beautiful – as a way of enabling clients to work through troubling situations in which they have found themselves in a more positive way, using the disappointment, shame, or anger arising from failure to lead to greater maturity and developmental potential for the individual within the organizational system.

Reading this book is therefore illuminating in creating another way of thinking about yourself in role and encourages you, the reader, to consider what unconscious influence family background might have had on authority and peer relationships, which, of course, is known subliminally but unknown until you consciously begin to think about it.

It is here that the 'unthought known' becomes useful: a concept developed by Christopher Bollas in his book *The Shadow of the Object: Psychoanalysis of the Unthought Known* – which refers to early, pre-verbal, and unconscious experiences that are known emotionally or physically but never consciously thought or formulated into words. It represents fundamental, sometimes traumatic, early life experiences that shape our adult personalities, behavior, and relationships.

In this way, the sense that past dynamics influence our behavior without us consciously knowing it can emerge through the work between the client and coach, and can cast light on the underlying dynamics affecting the client in their role and work environment, now including the 'unthought known' of the dynamics within the family of origin.

The many organizational stories that Francesca relates – about couples, founders, and siblings – show us how different facets of family life have a profound influence on current behaviour, especially at times of stress. She refers to different characteristics of family life including abusive, neglectful, incomplete, or absent families, and demonstrates how different characteristics of founder-parents, especially those with more narcissistic personality traits, have an unconscious impact on the later functioning of her clients. I found of particular interest her many examples of individuals struggling with their roles, their professional identities, and 'tribal' identifications.

More broadly, Francesca's examples of family business are fascinating. Here the family system and business system interlace, and this complexity need to be carefully managed, so that the individuals concerned are aware which role they are in when talking to a family member about the business. Questions of succession are clearly a thorny issue that needs careful consideration, especially as it is well known that such businesses can fail at the point of transition, and with the evidence showing that a high proportion of family businesses fail in the third generation, when the vision of the original founder no longer holds good.

Her examples highlight the importance of role awareness, boundaries, authority, and organization, and of how the family of origin 'in the mind' of the client generates feelings that need to be managed in the present work environment. In this way, she brings the inner world and the way we perform together, enabling clients to generate insights about the issues they face, and empowering them to implement meaningful solutions to what appeared originally to be intractable problems.

This book therefore contains many examples of success stories based on the work that Francesca has carried out with her clients, based on her capacity to challenge their current ways of operating whilst continuing to support them in their struggle for solutions.

I hope that the foregoing will encourage you to read this lively, engaging, and thought-provoking book.

Olya Khaleelee
Corporate psychologist, organizational consultant,
Chairwoman of OPUS: an Organisation for
Promoting the Understanding of Society

Acknowledgements

I am grateful to my wonderful editor Sue Lescelle, who has accompanied me in the journey of this book from its conception. Her skillful editing, warm encouragement, and unwavering support have provided the emotional and practical scaffolding for *Family at Work*.

A big thank you to Megan Meredith for her helpful comments and observations on my first draft – her input has been invaluable.

Thank you to my colleagues Sheila Damon, Tim Dartington, Olya Khaleelee, and Vega Roberts for the lively and rich discussions over the years. The depth of their consultancy practice, their interesting ideas, and sharp perspectives have been a great inspiration. The approach explored in *Family at Work* is rooted in those conversations.

And finally, thank you to my son, Luca Picardi, for his design of the cover.

A Note on Confidentiality

All names of the examples in this book are fictitious, and the identifying details have been changed to preserve anonymity.

Several case illustrations are composite descriptions of individuals or organizations presenting similar dynamics.

Introduction

Our families are our first organizations: the roles we are given in them and the roles we take shape who we are, and inform how we respond and engage with the environment we are in. From TV shows such as *Succession* and *the Crown* to the interactions of influential families in real life like the Trumps and the Windsors, the blur of business and family is increasingly part of the cultural conversation and public fascination.

Family at Work explores how our family experience – its joys, challenges, and difficulties – affects how we take up our roles and how family dynamics can be re-enacted in the workplace. Developing awareness and an understanding of how we project elements of our early experience in a work context can help to shift disruptive dynamics and allow us to be more ourselves, without feeling trapped in repeating family patterns.

In the chapters that follow, I use my extensive experience of working with individuals and organizations to disentangle the psychological and emotional dynamics behind different and contrasting stories.

The stories I tell, though highly disguised, are based on real family dilemmas – on anguish, disappointment, and personal tragedies, as well as drive, passion, and love – and their impact on my clients' roles and experience of their work environment. I have been profoundly moved, intrigued, and concerned when listening to their stories and have also felt, at times, doubtful about my capacity to help them. This book is both about my clients' and my own journey – the bumpy road we've shared. It has been deeply satisfying to see some of the shifts and transformations my clients have been able to make in their working lives as a result of the new insights we've gained together from revisiting their significant early experiences.

DOI: 10.4324/9781003613961-1

HOW FAMILY AFFECTS THE WORKPLACE

This book offers a framework for understanding family dynamics in the workplace and their impact on how people take up their role within it. To that end, it is divided into the following sections:

PART 1: THE BENIGN THIRD – AND THE ART OF 'KINTSUGI'

This first part of this book will focus on the consultancy space, my practice, and the concept of the *benign third* – where difficult conversations can take place. In this space, built on the mutual trust and engagement between client and consultant, it is possible to explore and disentangle disruptive family dynamics. It is here that 'the unthought known' (Bollas) – the sense that past dynamics influence our behaviour without consciously knowing it – can emerge and cast light on the underlying dynamics affecting the client in their role and work environment.

PART 2: FAMILY AT WORK

The main section of this book examines how different family roles and configurations, and early traumatic events or a lack of family, can shape and affect the way we are at work. It describes the journey of many leaders, professionals, and family businesses in their search to find a different way to engage with work without being trapped or too affected by their early family experiences.

Chapter 1. ***Family in the mind*** describes how we inevitably project unconscious family dynamics onto the workplace. Without realizing it, we can experience our boss as a father or mother figure or repeat sibling dynamics with our peers. These dynamics might be easily shaken off, or they could be hard to disentangle and make our relationships at work challenging.

Chapter 2. ***Couples at work*** explores couples' dynamics in family businesses, their feelings of rivalry and competition, as well as their desire for closeness, and differentiation in the context of loving relationships. It examines how ordinary dynamics become magnified in an environment where couples must constantly move between the private sphere and the business environment.

Chapter 3. ***Founders – proud or narcissistic parents?*** considers how a degree of narcissism might be essential in helping founders to believe in what they have created and protect it from the external world – how 'healthy' elements of narcissism can possibly strengthen confidence in oneself and in the creative endeavour, whereas 'unhealthy' narcissism could derail their journey.

Chapter 4. ***Family businesses*** explores the tensions and interplay between the two systems: the family system and the business system, and how different family businesses have dealt with these complexities and challenges.

Chapter 5. ***The challenge of succession – 'killing the father'*** describes the dynamics of succession in different organizations and family businesses – how the old and new generations have dealt with the process of endings and new beginnings. It also explores the role tribal dynamics play in the succession process.

Chapter 6. ***Siblings at work*** focuses on the challenges and complexities of working with peers, where the pleasure of sharing and collaborating with 'work siblings' is mixed up with feelings of rivalry and competition. It explores how our early experiences with siblings colour and influence our engagement with our work peers.

Chapter 7. ***Abusive families*** looks at how abusive dynamics in the workplace can create a climate of anxiety and a lack of trust. As a result, people can develop a dysfunctional attachment to their organization or leadership.

Chapter 8. ***The scar of an early loss*** draws on several different examples to explore the impact of an early loss on professional identity – the individuals described, all quite different, are linked by the premature loss of a member of their family and by the way this event has shaped their engagement with their career.

Chapter 9. ***We are not a family*** describes organizations or the departments within them that don't experience themselves as 'family' or are not perceived as 'blood relatives' – where there is a conscious or unconscious ambivalence about their legitimacy and the nature of their task.

Chapter 10. ***The absent family*** focusses on some people's experience of the absence of a deeper family bond – a lack of a containing environment in which to feel understood and supported in their growth and development.

Chapter 11. ***Falling out of love*** looks at the experience of separation or divorce from work coming to terms with their sense of betrayal for moving on and deviating from their original ideals, while also experiencing a great sense of relief and hope for a new chapter in their professional life.

Chapter 12. ***The grandparent effect*** examines how the wisdom and broader perspective acquired through experience can provide 'psychological containment' in work and societal settings – the 'grandparent effect' – despite a context where the value older people can bring to work, family, and society is often overlooked.

During the course of this book, I will refer to some concepts as a light theoretical scaffolding to my storytelling. The concepts I mention, such as the unthought known, projections, and attachment, have been key in helping me to understand the emotional context and dynamics of my clients' situations. I have therefore written a short glossary with references in the appendix of this book for readers who might be interested in knowing more about the theoretical framework behind this book (see page 116).

WHY THIS BOOK?

I have always been intrigued by the family patterns we have internalized and carry with us, how they re-emerge in many contexts and situations, sometimes unexpectedly, and how powerful their shadow can be.

Family can take many shapes and structures. Our internalized relationship with parental figures, siblings, step-families, and adoptive family members are at the core on how we develop our identity as adults.

I have listened to many organizational stories where family experiences have played a significant part in the ways in which people have engaged with their roles and their organization. I have noticed how in stressful circumstances, for example, old behavioural patterns can re-emerge, often creating strong feelings and reactions – something I have experienced myself, in my own response to organizational dynamics and challenges.

People's capacity for making the link and acknowledging the resurfacing of family dynamics can be transformational and allow them to learn how to distinguish between family and work, without denying the inevitable overlap and the draw to repeat 'familiar' patterns.

As the eldest daughter of two, I have experienced myself the pressures and privileges of being the first child: the sense of responsibility as well as the desire, conscious and unconscious, to be and to do better than my younger sister, and to be bolder, more authoritative, and thoughtful. A competitive edge that I had to learn to manage rather than hide.

I grew up in a family of well-integrated 'outsiders', where the influence of my charismatic English grandmother and very liberal and open-minded parents in a conservative and provincial Italian town made me feel quite different and slightly on the outside. This possibly lay behind my avoidance of pursuing a career within an organization and gave me instead an appetite for taking roles at the boundaries of organizations – though still not without some longing to be fully inside them.

I moved country at a time when that was still quite unusual in my circle of friends. Later, I came to realize this was a way of reconnecting with the roots of my English grandmother – who had been a strong presence in my childhood – and that my desire to be different originated both with my family's liberal outlook, and my generation's aspiration not to conform to traditional expectations. However, writing my second book in English isn't just an attempt to show off retrospectively to my English grandmother or my perfectly bilingual mother, who never taught me the language; rather, it is a touchstone of the life and family I have since built for myself in Britain. Reflecting on and unpacking my own family background, and my role within it, has given me a deeper understanding of how to manage the repetition and enactment of unhelpful dynamics from the past in my own professional role and work contexts – what Freud called repetition compulsion: our tendency to repeat a difficult or traumatic event from the past, often without realizing we are doing it.

Family is something we all have, in whatever form. Whether we like it or not, it affects our lives at home and at work. However, we shouldn't feel imprisoned by it. We can try to understand and manage the impact it has on us and learn to spot when we are repeating unhelpful and potentially disrupting behaviours.

This book is for people in a work role, both inside and outside organizations, who are curious about their own response to their work environment and interested to develop their understanding of the dynamics at play. It is also for leaders, consultants, and coaches who wish to develop a deeper understanding of the dynamics below the surface affecting their staff and clients.

I hope readers will be able to identify with the scenarios I describe or apply insights gleaned from them to their own situations. The stories I share are based on real clients, although I have changed many details to preserve confidentiality. Several vignettes are a mixture of different situations, which presented very similar dynamics. Some of the key ideas and concepts discussed in this book also relate to my previous book *Work Matters, Consulting to Leaders and Organizations in the Tavistock Tradition*. The two books are complementary.

Part 1

The Benign Third – the Art of 'Kintsugi'

Work can be a source of great pleasure as well as of profound distress. It can provide a setting for creativity, influence, and meaningful social interactions, or be a frustrating, and difficult place, where we feel unable to fulfil our potential or realize our expectations.

Work also represents our capacity to invest in something away from our immediate environment, beyond our individuality, family, and community. In a fast-changing world with its constant technological innovations, such as AI, in which organizations are becoming progressively less containing, our work identity is becoming very central, relating more directly to our core competencies as individuals than to an organization. And the boundaries between our work identity and our personal identity are becoming increasingly fluid.

When I meet my clients, they're usually in a phase of transition and flux, or they feel discouraged, stuck, and unhappy in their role or in their organization. Approaching someone about consultancy takes courage: you need to be prepared to share complex, confusing, and painful experiences and learn to trust the process. It requires a jump into an unknown and experimental zone.

Sometimes this isn't possible – something doesn't click into place to enable the process of discovery to occur. The individual or the group might not be emotionally ready, too anxious about the 'unknown' or too defensive about the possibility of taking responsibility for what isn't working.

However, the stories I share in this book, though differing in context, personalities, and challenges, are all about people who were able to take that leap and embrace this way of working. The approach I describe in *Family at Work* became a significant element in their journey: the capacity to identify and engage with dynamics under the surface, the 'subterranean stream', and to make connections between the conscious and unconscious elements of their experience. It's often a bumpy ride that requires the capacity, on both sides, not to rush into solutions, instead staying in the uncertainty of the moment and letting some of the key dynamics emerge gradually.

DOI: 10.4324/9781003613961-2

I see myself as being a 'benign third' in this process: someone who listens, engages, makes links, and tries not to be judgemental. At times, it requires effort and humility to acknowledge that the material brought to me by my clients has stirred up something in me, allowing myself to be 'contaminated' by the client's dynamics and recognizing my own difficulties in order to engage with them. For example, I remember the time when a colleague and I were consulting to a wealthy family business. We felt quite disapproving towards the family, somehow 'above' the rivalry among the siblings about inheritance and money.

Later, in our staff debrief, my colleague and I started to make some connections with our own family dynamics and issues about money. 'My siblings couldn't accept my grandfather left me some money and did everything they could to put a stop to it. I couldn't forgive them for years,' my colleague said.

Old feelings of envy and disappointment re-emerged, and we were able to connect this to our clients' experience and become more tuned in to the complexities of their feelings, and more empathic to their situation. As this example illustrates, we needed to feel 'contaminated' or affected enough by our clients' dynamics to be properly engaged with them and capable of helping them to address their own situation and painful feelings. Like an anthropologist immersing herself in a different culture, I try to immerse myself in my client's environment, observing patterns and dynamics while suspending judgement and beliefs.

I try to capture and understand the dynamics under the surface in individuals and organizations, as well as pay attention to the systemic elements connected to their situations.

THE ART OF ACKNOWLEDGING IMPERFECTION

The Japanese use a technique called *kintsugi* to restore broken ceramic pieces, whereby they mix lacquer with powdered gold. The golden lacquer highlights the cracks instead of concealing them; both the break and the repair become part of the story of an object instead of something that needs to be hidden. The repaired object can even become more beautiful than the original, giving it another life.

Kintsugi can act as a metaphor for the consultancy process too, whereby difficulties, misjudgements, and disappointments come to the surface and are explored. The work together, with its insights, challenges and discoveries, provides the gold powder for the reparation process without attempting to conceal the cracks and wounds that have emerged. In the following stories, I will try to convey how the *kintsugi* technique, when translated into the consultancy process, offers opportunities for transformation and growth – the creation of a 'new chapter' complete with golden cracks.

CREATING A NEW NARRATIVE

Through telling me their stories, individuals revisit and reframe key personal and professional events. But it's the narrative we create together that provides the opportunity for fresh insights and new connections, the gold powder that will eventually glue together their personal and professional journey and the uneven patterns that have shaped and coloured their experiences.

It can be challenging to revisit our well-established view of ourselves, recognize our defensive structures, and understand the connection between a current work problem and a dynamic originating in our early years.

I remember when I had a similar revelation in my late twenties, when I started analysis. I was talking about my younger sister and remembering how protective I felt towards her; I described how I'd even stood in front of her pram to prevent people 'disturbing' her when she was asleep… For the first time, in telling my story to my analyst, I realized how jealous I'd been and how much I wanted people to look at me rather than her. It was a significant insight that helped me to understand my feelings of resentment and rivalry towards my sister, still very much alive after so many years.

More recently, in a consultancy setting, my client Ben told me about his lack of confidence at work, despite his abilities and successful career. The only child of his mother's second marriage and the first member of his family to go to university, he had embraced a successful career in finance, yet found himself growing progressively distant from his half-siblings and parents. He had moved to a different country, ostensibly to broaden his experience and make a fresh start. However, he was now feeling lost and disorientated.

He described how his profession, high salary, and change of 'class' had created a rift between him and his original family, who seemed resentful and possibly envious of his achievements. Ben felt the loss of his relationship with his siblings, with whom he had been very close when he was growing up. The loss of his 'tribe' had a strong impact on his work identity, too. He struggled to connect with his peers and kept his distance from most of his colleagues, fearing and avoiding forming closer relationships with them. Though technically very able, he lacked confidence in social interactions.

While telling me his story, Ben started to make some significant connections. The *unthought known* (as described by Bollas) – an emotional sense that a past dynamic influences our behaviour without consciously acknowledging or knowing what this is – began to emerge: he could see the disturbing impact that his moving 'up' into the professional class had had on his relationship with his family. Their inability to address this dynamic had a profound impact on his identity and on his ability to create meaningful new relationships both inside and outside work. Though the realization was painful, Ben felt relieved he could now join together the dots that connected his current situation with his life story. The new narrative created the texture for a deeper understanding of what was at play and the opportunity to regain some agency over his future choices.

Unlike Ben, Tristan came from a very privileged background. The eldest son of very wealthy landowners, he had been expected to be involved in the family estate from an early age. Still, he'd felt out of place and had decided to step away by moving to the States and starting to build a career as a film producer. However, a few years later, his father suddenly died, and he felt he had to go back to the family business.

We met around that time, which was a period of confusion for Tristan, when he didn't know who he was or what he wanted. He was experiencing a mixture of resentment and resignation.

'I loved my family,' he told me, 'but I couldn't contemplate the prospect of missing out on the opportunity of trying something different, new, and creative. It felt very liberating, though the guilt of having abandoned the family business never left me.'

A powerful internal voice kept telling him he hadn't earned his role in the family business, while at the same time he'd missed out on opportunities to be independent and entrepreneurial and strike out beyond the influence of his family and background.

The focus of our work together was to create a new narrative in which his privileged situation could be put to good use, rather than be a source of unease or resentment – a place where he could begin to engage in new creative ventures. Gradually, Tristan started to connect and integrate his two identities more – those of the privileged son and the creative entrepreneur – without feeling too concerned or guilty about the advantages of his family situation or too aggrieved by the loss of his career as a film producer.

His affection for his family and attachment to the estate where he grew up were the glue that helped him in this journey. He started to refurbish some old cottages on the estate for holiday lets and social events. The project was ambitious and was initially viewed by his family with a degree of scepticism. However, Tristan kept his nerve and was able to launch his new initiative after a couple of years.

My role as a 'benign third' was to accompany him through the different stages of the project, creating a space where he could express his doubts and anxiety. Together, we developed a new narrative where his situation and desires for the future could be explored from a fresh perspective. In the *kintsugi* tradition, his feelings and underlying emotions were made visible with a 'dust of gold'.

Tristan has now developed a thriving business. His cottages have also been used for film locations, creating a bridge with the world he left behind. Part of our work together was also to establish clearer boundaries with his family, helping him to separate his family roles from his professional ones – a constant challenge for family businesses.

The two systems, family and business, often overlap, creating emotional confusion and anxiety about the impact on relationships in both domains (see chapter on family businesses). Problems with boundaries often lie at the root of misunderstandings and disappointments about roles or tasks. Difficulties with boundaries are also at the core of my following stories.

DILEMMAS ABOUT BOUNDARIES

Boundaries are tricky: many people struggle to strike the right emotional distance from their colleagues, bosses and employees, and can get into difficulties by becoming too involved and too close to them, or too distant and formal, all of which can make a relationship more challenging and complicated. I'm not talking here about romantic or sexual liaisons, but something more subtle – from the idealization of a boss to a close friendship with a colleague, or a lack of flexibility and empathy.

Boundaries are also a central element in the consultancy setting. The relationships I develop with my clients are quite intimate; I get to know their dilemmas and difficulties in depth. I often identify strongly with some of my clients' challenges, feel empathy for their problems and, at times, get drawn into taking 'their side'. It can also be tempting to be too familiar with them, at risk of creating confusion about our roles.

Keeping firm boundaries in place is key to providing a safe space and a critical stance. My clients, showing a desire for a closer and friendlier relationship, might unconsciously invite me to 'collude' with their unconscious wish not to change or to hide their shortcomings. I might be experienced as potentially threatening as well as potentially helpful; or I might feel the pressure not to challenge the status quo and unconsciously collude with my client's ambivalence and wish not to change.

Maintaining firm boundaries, though with warmth and understanding and creating a space sufficiently intimate yet sufficiently distant, is essential for the process of discovery and exploration to take place. It also provides a template, a 'role model' for those people who struggle to maintain the right emotional distance from colleagues and bosses at work, which brings me to Mark's story.

Mark was in awe of Patrick, the professor who was head of his department. He had known him before joining the faculty; Patrick had been a consultant for his previous organization. He had been impressed by his charm, charisma, and knowledge. When Mark left the organization, he felt flattered to be asked to join Patrick's faculty, where he was quickly promoted to a senior role. Patrick and Mark often socialized in the evenings after running demanding programmes together. He met his family and felt very included in his world – part of his inner circle. He confided, 'I used to be invited to their summer parties in their country home – I was the only one invited from our faculty…'

When Patrick developed a new prestigious course, Mark was expecting to lead it himself. Instead, Patrick chose Claire, Mark's ambitious and competitive colleague. It was quite a blow. Old familiar feelings of exclusion remerged, and Mark felt unfairly put aside.

When we unpacked this situation together, the blurring of boundaries became quite evident – the confusion between professional relationship and friendship, and particularly his strong desire to be the 'chosen' one. He could recognize how he longed to be chosen and how he had looked for Patrick's approval in his new career.

Mark's complex relationship with his siblings, the underlying sense that he was never fully 'noticed' and his desire for approval and recognition had an interesting connection to the dynamic with Patrick. His experience of feeling excluded and overlooked brought back echoes from his past. The confusion around boundaries added to the problem. Mark didn't see this incident as just unfortunate or disappointing, something you might expect to happen in a work context. For him, this was a betrayal of a friendship, as well as confirmation of his feelings of never being fully 'seen' and appreciated.

As a result of our work together, Mark became more aware of the many elements that led to his strong reaction and stressful experience. The blurring of boundaries had weakened his position and agency in his role within the faculty. Gradually, he regained his confidence and was able to redraw some clearer boundaries with Patrick, resisting the original temptation to slam the door and leave the department.

Mark had also felt publicly 'shamed' in relation to the faculty through losing the leading role to a less experienced and less capable colleague, a strong emotion that we'll consider later on.

The blurring of boundaries in my next story is more extreme, showing the consequences of not paying enough attention to the need to separate the personal and professional spheres.

BLURRING THE BOUNDARIES

Laura, a young, bright, and attractive young woman, never went to university. She charmed her way into the working world helped by her looks, versatility, and family connections. She became the chief executive officer (CEO), and partner of a start-up in the fashion industry. This venture was the brainchild of a couple, Louis and Alan, who had worked for years in the same fashion house and wanted now to branch out and create their own company. Laura, with her youth, charm, and natural elegance, seemed the perfect face for the organization. She was also well connected and had brought money into the business from her family and from another investor.

She came to see me after the initial honeymoon period with Louis, and Alan was starting to show some cracks. She was feeling quite isolated and lonely, an 'intruder' into a very close relationship. She had been initially adopted by the couple, spending a lot of time at their house and meeting their friends and families. She loved their lifestyle, their parties, and warm hospitality.

As an only child who had been quite indulged by her family, Laura missed her parents, who had relocated to France, and she had found in Louis and Alan both a surrogate family and a new exciting career. However, their relation had become increasingly incestuous, with a blurring of boundaries between their social life and work life, preventing her from taking up her CEO role properly. A daughter rather than a partner, she often felt undermined or overlooked and that she lacked the authority to take decisions. She thought the two partners were running the show, while she was treated and seen as just an extra.

There was also another issue or secret that came up in our conversations, which was becoming increasingly problematic:

Laura was having a secret affair with the main financial investor. Nobody else knew about it or seemed to suspect it. At the beginning of their relationship, he was very relaxed about his 'gift' to the company, but now that their relationship was coming to an end, he wasn't sure he wanted to keep his investment in a company that wasn't doing particularly well, but which was still struggling to make an impact in a very competitive market.

The breaking and blurring of boundaries was thus two-fold: with the two partners there was a confusion between their friendship system and their business system, resulting in Laura feeling lacking in authority and unable to take up her CEO role; while the secret relationship with the investor was potentially putting the business at risk. It was a mess!

Laura was very reluctant to tell her partners about the relationship, fearing their disapproval. However, I did wonder if Alan and Louis already knew about the affair, but chose to turn a blind eye to it to protect the financial gain for their company. They all seemed wrapped up in a phantasy that confusion and haziness about boundaries wasn't a real issue – just something they could easily navigate without significant consequences. Seduction, charm, and a desire to please each other were at the centre of their difficulties in acquiring the rigour, discipline and structure necessary to grow a sound business.

I don't know the end of this story. Laura couldn't commit to the coaching process, and we only had a few sessions together. She used the space to unburden, share her secret, and start to sketch what could happen next. She realized she had gone too far in her lack of boundaries and could see the potential risks for the business from her relationship with the investor. Yet taking a more thoughtful approach to her situation without relying on her charm and seductiveness was a struggle.

When we first met I, too, had been charmed by Laura's apparent openness, liveliness, and innovative thinking. In hindsight, I realized I had a taste of what she was like with other people and how easy it could be to overlook her difficulties in being fully engaged and focussed.

The possibility of being 'shamed' was perhaps behind Laura keeping her relationship secret, which I will be exploring next.

SHAME

Shame is a powerful feeling that can provoke strong emotional consequences in the working environment. Moreover, the powerful emotions that a sense of failure can stir up in individuals are often enhanced by dysfunctional and disruptive organizational dynamics.

Paul Hoggett distinguishes between depressive shame and paranoid shame:

> Depressive shame is a quite healthy emotion because it might lead us to be disappointed with ourselves and therefore resolved to address our failures and meet our goals and ideals… Paranoid shame might be a much more corrosive feeling of humiliation where one feels just not good enough… where failure means uselessness.
>
> (Hoggett, 2017)

In a work context, shame affects both the organization and the individual: it is the possibility of shame that leads organizations to act too hastily and get rid of 'the bad apple' without thinking; and it is the shame of being seen to do something wrong or to be experienced as inadequate that contributes to the collapse of confidence and competence in the individuals involved. The public nature of working in an organization makes us more exposed to humiliation and vulnerable to shame. The challenge for organizations and individuals is to shift from persecutory shame to depressive shame, accepting shame as, at times, an unescapable ingredient in the complexity of organizational life – and to be able to feel ashamed without disintegrating under the gaze of other people. As the following story shows, the narcissistic wound of being 'shamed' or publicly criticized is hard to heal.

Harish, a senior cardiologist, was accused of harassing junior staff. He had an impeccable clinical record, and the medical director was reluctant to suspend him. Instead, he was instructed to take a period of leave and have some coaching to help him review and address his behaviour.

Harish came from a family of doctors; medicine was in his DNA. He had had a formal upbringing and a quite distant father, an 'old school' surgeon. He felt different from his father, more tuned in to his patients and was very dedicated to his discipline and practice. The incident that provoked the complaint was indeed related to his concern for a patient. He'd snapped at a nurse who performed a clinical procedure wrongly, causing the patient some unnecessary pain. He couldn't tolerate poor performance, particularly with very ill and frail patients.

He explained, 'I could see the patient was suffering – something that wouldn't have happened with a more competent nurse. I felt very angry and disappointed.'

Harish felt bruised by and ashamed of the accusations of harassment and struggled to understand how he'd reached this point. When we first met, we were interrupted by a call from his wife who asked how he was getting on with me. It showed how anxious he must have felt about this process and how challenging it was for him to discuss his role and current difficulties with me.

It took some time for a new narrative to emerge, which enabled him to identify what lay behind his approach to work. His old-fashioned upbringing and internalized leadership model, which was quite rigid and clinically focussed, prevented him from seeing the bigger picture and developing a more empathic approach towards junior staff. Harish also struggled to understand that his age, position, and clinical excellence intimidated people and made them quite anxious around him.

We discussed what it meant to be able to be critical in a way that could be heard and the importance of debriefing his staff regularly, giving the team the time in which to discuss near misses and mistakes. We also looked at how his clinical focus shouldn't prevent him from being emotionally present with his team and his responsibility to lead this process.

Harish started to engage with this perspective, although he wouldn't commit to long-term coaching. The narcissistic wound of having risked suspension and the shame of being 'disciplined' got in the way of his doing further work on his approach. The experience was probably too painful for him. He couldn't fully appreciate the potential benefits of a *kintsugi* approach in which the cracks could be seen and not disguised.

When Harish was referred to me, I made it clear that his case shouldn't be looked at in isolation. The organization, I suggested, might have been complicit through avoiding the need to confront the consultant about his leadership approach much earlier on. His reputation as an excellent clinician, and his status within the hospital meant the leadership had turned a blind eye for a long time.

This is not unusual. It's easier to identify an individual as the 'guilty' party without acknowledging the organization's role in the situation. Alternatively, sometimes a person may 'act out' an organizational dynamic that it's more acceptable for the organization to attribute to an individual, as shown in the story that follows.

THE INDIVIDUAL AND THE SYSTEM

Martin was the head of administration in a busy clinic for children and families. He was known for his empathic and supportive approach to the clinic's clients. He always went the extra mile to explain processes and procedures to anxious parents and was warm and welcoming towards their children.

Nevertheless, the clinicians themselves had mixed feelings about the administrative team: on the one hand, they felt highly dependent on them and their support; on the other, they were uneasy about the 'familiar' approach the admin team took with the clinic's clients. They also felt quite jealous about the freedom and flexibility enjoyed by the admin team, without the rigidity of their own professional boundaries. For their part, the admin team, though aware of the huge pressure on the clinicians, felt somewhat excluded from key decisions and resented the notion that they were somehow considered 'second-class citizens' or, as someone put it, not 'blood relatives'.

At a team meeting, Martin referred in passing to a conversation with a family: without realizing it, he shared critical information that should have been discussed first with the clinicians. People were stunned by this breach of confidentiality and Martin felt bruised and shamed as a result. In the subsequent consultancy session, people shared their strong feelings of mistrust and disappointment in each other. The split between the admin system and the clinical system became even more apparent.

I suggested that Martin's incident wasn't just related to his lack of judgement and a desire to reassure a family. It was evidence of a lack of integration between the two systems. Through a role-play in which each group played the 'other' team, they unpacked their prejudices and rigid positions more clearly. This transitional and lighter space – there were a lot of jokes and much laughter about the caricatures of each other's roles: the 'self-important' clinicians and 'never available' administrators – provided an opportunity for the cracks to emerge and allowed the process of change to begin, with the golden powder starting to 'mend' those cracks.

These stories illustrate how the *kintsugi* approach can work if individuals and teams feel ready to undertake this bumpy journey, and the consultant is prepared to engage with the work without feeling under pressure to provide quick solutions or wanting to cover the cracks. It requires openness, humility, and a desire for truth from all parties.

Understanding the connection between a current work issue and a dynamic originating in our early years can help us to manage aspects of ourselves that have had a disruptive impact on our working lives. We might finally shift a behaviour belonging to the past that we have felt compelled to repeat.

The role of the benign third provides a sense of perspective and containment that can help to untangle entrenched and painful dynamics.

Like a distant though beloved relative or a trusted family friend, he or she can offer the emotional space needed to look at complex and painful situations afresh.

In the first chapter of Part 2, I describe the powerful effect that 'family in the mind' can have on our work roles – like an invisible shadow that follows us around, which can suddenly be activated in stressful and challenging situations. Then, in the chapters that follow, we'll take a closer look at how some of the different dynamics within families can play out in the workplace and the effect of these.

Part 2

Family at Work

CHAPTER 1

Family in the Mind

We inevitably project unconscious family dynamics in the workplace. Without realizing it, we can experience our boss as a father or mother figure or repeat sibling dynamics with our peers. These dynamics can be easily shaken off, or they can be hard to disentangle and make our relationships at work more challenging. They can accompany us like faint shadows and pop up without warning when we least expect them. An unpleasant incident at work or in a professional relationship can suddenly provoke a deep upset, a surprising rivalry, or profound empathy – powerful feelings connected to our own family history and dynamics. We can also recreate, without realizing it, a version of our family's structure and dynamics in the organizations and teams we lead.

Our family background might be a source of strength and inspiration, or, alternatively, it could be perceived as an inescapable cage – where we feel unconsciously compelled to repeat unhelpful or dysfunctional behaviours that we've experienced in a family context.

Despite their different situations, diverse contexts, and organizations, the stories I describe in this chapter all share the power and influence of the original imprint of the individual's family dynamics – a highly emotional template that re-emerges when people find themselves in particularly stressful and demanding circumstances.

Like our DNA, *family in the mind* plays its part in the way an individual responds to challenging and difficult situations. In other instances, *family in the mind* provides a functioning model that informs how the individual takes up their role – such as in Leila's case (below) and her leadership approach under the shadow of the patriarchal model of her family firm.

As discussed in Part 1, consultancy can help to identify and disentangle these dynamics and manage expectations, desires, and disappointments derived from our family's roles and history in our lives.

In this chapter, I have chosen examples that convey the strong impact of primary family dynamics on the work experience, including loss and death,

DOI: 10.4324/9781003613961-4

parental love and patriarchy, lack of belonging, difference, and finally abandonment and neglect. All the individuals I describe have been impaired in their roles, often unconsciously, by the subtle but powerful effect of these early experiences.

A vivid illustration of these dynamics is, for example, when the experience of death in the workplace becomes a very powerful emotional trigger, taking us back to our personal experiences and overwhelming emotions, as Josh's story demonstrates.

A SHARED SENSE OF LOSS

Josh was the leader of a university postgraduate programme. He was highly revered by his students for his charm and innovative approach.

When he unexpectedly lost his adolescent daughter, who'd had mental health problems for several years and eventually took her own life, Josh's colleagues arranged to meet the students to inform them of the sad event and create a space for people to express their sorrow and condolences.

The tutors were expecting an emotional meeting, but nothing had prepared them for such an intense outpouring of feelings: people reacted to the news as if Josh's daughter were their own child, sister, or closest friend – many were tearful and openly distressed. It seemed almost impossible to distinguish between the tragic loss experienced by their teacher and their own experience of this terrible event.

Their disproportionate reaction might also have been heightened by Josh having shared his concerns about his daughter with them beforehand – interestingly, without revealing any of this to his colleagues – creating the impression of a special bond with the students. However, it was something he shouldn't have disclosed or discussed with them in his role as their teacher and leader of the programme. (See the section on boundaries in Part 1, page XX.)

It took a while for the tutors to help the students to come back to reality and recognize that the young girl's death was an incredibly sad incident, but it wasn't their own personal loss.

'It's a very upsetting situation – hard to imagine how Josh must be feeling at this moment – though it's not your daughter who died. Despite our sorrow for Josh, we should carry on with our work', one of the tutors said to the students.

The students had projected onto her death their experiences of other significant deaths in their own personal lives, losing their sense of perspective. Their *family in the mind* had been mobilized and had generated very strong emotional reactions in them, which were difficult to contain and manage. The close relationship they had developed with Josh made them feel like part of his family for a moment and experience the pain he was experiencing.

In the following story, the *family in the mind* takes a different shape and shows the powerful effect of a patriarchal model on my client's approach to her role as leader.

A PATRIARCHAL MODEL

Leila, the daughter of a successful businessman, had been involved in the family company since graduation. Despite her talents and commitment to the firm, she had been relegated to a secondary role. However, she didn't appear to resent the fact that her brothers had much more prominent positions in the company – mainly because she adored and idealized her father: in her eyes, he could do no wrong. Her father had grown his business from nothing, creating a well-respected professional services organization and providing the whole family with a very comfortable living.

Nevertheless, this role wasn't enough for Leila. She started to get involved with Vale – a non-profit organization for disabled children and their families – in a parallel career. The founder of Vale was an inspiring and charismatic leader who had created an innovative, community-centred organization, providing care, support, and hope to a very complex and demanding client group. When he suddenly died after a brief illness, Leila felt mobilized to step in, becoming the leader of the organization. It was an interesting step up: she took up the leadership role she was denied in her family business.

Her original attraction to Vale was driven by her desire to balance the highly commercial focus of her family business with charitable work and, I suspect, by the familiarity of the founder's leadership style – a patriarchal approach that encouraged a strong transference towards their leader in exchange for protection and validation.

Her approach and understanding of the organizational dynamics were inevitably influenced by her experience of her own family's firm with her father at the helm. Leila experienced the patriarchal approach – 'the rule of the father' – as a benign leadership model, despite it having contributed to keeping her side-lined in both organizations.

She said, 'I always felt very protective towards Dad, even when I didn't agree with his choices, which rarely happened. I knew he always meant well and wanted to look after all of us – our family and the employees'.

As a woman who had never been in a leadership role before, Leila handled her new position with great caution, almost as if she were only standing in for the venerated leader and waiting for a similar charismatic figure to turn up. The way Vale was organized was never challenged and she made very few changes. I often wondered if, in Leila's mind, Vale's former leader, like her father, could do no wrong.

She approached me two years into the role, when she felt stressed by increasing turbulence among the staff and challenging new demands from the external environment. Despite her insights and thoughtfulness, there was an underlying resistance to 'touch' the organizational model, even if there was plenty of evidence that Vale needed to make substantial changes to remain relevant and sustainable. The *patriarchal model* in the mind acted as a strait-jacket, preventing Leila, the dutiful daughter, from taking up her authority and leading according to her own style and the current organizational needs and challenges. It took many conversations between us for her to unpick this internal dynamic and recognize the patriarchal imprint, so difficult to leave behind – as if 'touching' the organizational model and initiating some innovations represented a betrayal of the paternal authority.

Leila has now finally started to make some changes, developing the leadership team, introducing a deputy role, and making the staff more accountable for their work and behaviour. While she still proceeds with caution, she acts with more determination and clarity. She used to struggle with trusting her intuition and insights into what needed to be done. It was the possibility of the business closing or having to make drastic cuts that finally helped her to assume authority and take up her leadership role more fully. As I said to her, she was learning to translate her insights into actions.

Ultimately, she is now making her organization more like a business than a family (see chapter on family businesses).

While Leila's issues related to the precedent set by her father, the following story focusses on how a *refugee family in the mind* coloured Zuri's experience of her first leadership role.

ALWAYS A REFUGEE...

Zuri, elegant and very tall, makes an immediate impression of someone at ease in her own skin – confident and clever. She speaks perfect English with just a slight accent that adds to her charm.

A few months ago, she became the chief executive officer (CEO) of Futureland, an organization focussing on climate change and environmental issues. She is passionate about its work and determined to increase the pressure on the government to implement and develop progressive policies on the environment and the effect of climate change.

Despite the full backing of her appointment from the board and the initial positive response from the executive team, she now finds herself facing several challenges from both inside and outside the organization. People have responded to her bold approach and initial attempts at introducing some radical changes with scepticism and passive resistance.

Futureland had been stagnant for many years under its original founder, who had progressively lost his edge and focus. Staff and sponsors had complained, implicitly, and explicitly, about this uninspiring situation for a long time, so Zuri's appointment was initially seen as a breath of fresh air and a real opportunity for change and development. However, they now felt anxious about the future and had started questioning her capacity to transform the organization.

The staff and sponsors' doubts and anxieties were echoed strongly in Zuri's own thoughts. Despite her impeccable credentials and sharp intellect, she had started to feel uncertain about her ability to take up this challenging leadership role. It's at this point that she started to look for help; she understood she needed another perspective – that of someone who could help to unravel what was behind her sudden lack of confidence and sense of overwhelm.

Zuri's story, as the only daughter of a single mother who came to UK with nothing and very little education or English, is quite extraordinary. She managed to complete her studies, performing brilliantly at both school and university, while looking after her mother, who suffered from several serious illnesses. Now, with a career behind her as a distinguished scientist, married with two young children, and living in an up-and-coming area in London, she seems to have reached a point thousand miles away from her first arrival in UK. Still, the *refugee in the mind* pops up under the pressure of her new demanding role, as if the original imprint were threatening her actual status and perception of herself.

Her difference, which she has proudly emphasized and, at times, even used as a selling point in the past, was coming back at her like a boomerang. The experience of her complex personal history and struggles, instead of adding value and providing original perspectives to her role, was now making her feel insecure and alone – a deep-seated sense of not belonging, shared by many people whose circumstances have dramatically changed from where they started out.

Though taken by surprise by her powerful emotional response, she has known all along that the *refugee* shadow is always with her – the fear of hunger, of going back to the gutter and never being in a secure place. Something other people could detect and possibly exploit, perhaps even without realizing it; similar to how Elisabeth Strout's character Lucy Barton puts it, it was as though people could smell she belonged to the underclass.

Like many other refugees, Zuri was feeling an ambivalent attachment to the context she was in (see attachment, page 00), lacking the experience of a secure psychological environment so fundamental for healthy development and integration.

This experience was heightened by an element of hubris – her immense pride in her successful journey through such tempestuous waters – as if she were somehow above most of the people around her. Her refugee status was thus double-edged, creating a myth of strength, focus, and determination, but also with an emerging shadow side – a sense of loss, insecurity, and lack of a firm base.

It took many months for Zuri to come to terms with her double-edged refugee's state of mind and acknowledge its profound effect on the way she engaged with her leadership role. Though she was devoted to her mother, she felt the lack of a family and the absence of roots that could ground her into her community and society. The refugee template in her mind coloured her response to stressful situations as if she had no country and family of her own, the feeling of being alone against the world.

'This feeling of loneliness and lack of roots is like a volcano: it could erupt at any time, without a warning', Zuri whispered during one of our sessions together.

Through our consultation, Zuri became aware of her internal dynamics and conflicted feelings and was able to take significant steps to moderate and balance her approach. She realized that, as a leader, she had to take people with her. The changes she wanted to implement had to happen at a pace her staff and sponsors could manage. She couldn't go at the fast pace she was used to in her personal life and previous career, driven by her strong will to succeed. She had felt then that she couldn't afford to waste time, in case someone found out where she came from.

She also recognized that her wish to be viewed as extraordinary needed to be moderated. Being more ordinary didn't mean she had to surrender rigour and her drive for positive change; instead, it could contribute to her taking people with her on the organization's journey.

In the last story in this chapter, the family in the mind concerns a neglectful family, affecting Bill's capacity to trust parental figures in his organization.

THE NEGLECTFUL FAMILY

Bill, a bright senior executive, had enjoyed a successful career with Benvenuto, an organization in the hospitality sector, which had been his professional home for almost 15 years. The organization had started out as a family business and had now become a global company, offering interesting and diverse career paths for its employees. Bill had come to me as part of a company scheme that offered coaching to senior executives, with the objective of supporting them in their leading roles and exploring different possible avenues for the next chapters of their careers.

I was quite excited to learn more about this organizational world – an industry I knew very little about, and where I had only ever been a customer. It was quite disappointing, then, to realize that Bill was a very concrete thinker, lacking the imagination and liveliness of many of my clients. I struggled to engage fully with his situation. There was an emotional distance in the way he related to me and to his role, and an underlying depressive streak that I failed to detect in our first sessions.

Yet today's session was different. Bill seemed changed, clearly upset, and agitated. His usual courteous and quite distant veneer had been smashed by very powerful feelings. He looked tired and dishevelled, as if he hadn't slept for days. He explained that his boss, who he rated highly, had encouraged him to apply for a more senior position on the understanding that he would be the most suitable candidate. However, in the end, his boss had chosen Josie, a younger and less experienced colleague. It was, Bill says, a public humiliation, as everybody expected him to get the role and now wondered why he failed to do so.

Did Bill have any skeletons in his wardrobe?

Very good at school and university, Bill wasn't used to failure. His track record within the company was excellent, and he couldn't believe this had happened to him. He felt betrayed by his 'adopted family'. It was as if his whole professional world had collapsed. In particular, he felt hurt by his boss's betrayal, the parental figure he valued and who he'd thought also valued him.

'Parents can't be trusted... I know that only too well', he said now.

Though his reaction was partly understandable, the intensity and power of his feelings were evidence of deeper dynamics at play. I wondered what he meant by 'parents can't be trusted', as I knew very little about his family background.

He described how he hadn't experienced an ordinary childhood with his mother, who was a member of a strict religious sect, and a very distant father. He used to accompany his mother door to door to preach her religious beliefs, while his father lived elsewhere and wasn't involved in Bill's life. University saved Bill, and he created his own life and family, far removed from his parents and his original home.

Interestingly, he had developed a surrogate family in his work environment and had started to trust his boss as a benign parental figure. When he wasn't chosen for the new role, the *neglectful family in the mind* suddenly re-emerged – something he had managed to keep at a distance for a very long time. He felt neglected and betrayed by his professional family. This episode, that might have provoked disappointment and anger in others, became a tragedy to Bill.

I realized that my own initial boredom and difficulty in engaging with him were signs of my unconscious reaction to the underlying depression he had been carrying with him for many years.

My experience of boredom was a sign that something wasn't right, though it took me a while to engage with that feeling and understand what lay behind it. I was probably resisting being contaminated by his underlying depression;

initially, it was easier for me to go along with Bill in a more superficial way, and to avoid confronting his deeper unhappiness.

Through our work together, we were able to explore his distress and huge disappointment: Bill started to understand the connection between his family history and his expectations of himself and others. His intense disenchantment with his boss as parental figure became more manageable, and Bill started to look for other jobs inside and outside his organization.

Though my intervention helped Bill to move on and to re-engage with his situation in a constructive way, it wasn't my role to dig much further into his personal life. I did encourage him to explore the possibility of therapy, to work through the trauma of his early life and make him more equipped to face the emotional impact of similar situations in the future. As in other cases, when personal and family traumas haven't been worked through, making the individual vulnerable to primitive dynamics and very difficult feelings, coaching might not be enough.

However, Bill chose not to go to therapy, having recovered his confidence and his sense of value. He felt the work we have done together was sufficient for the time being. I remained doubtful about this, as I wasn't sure he would be able to sustain his more positive outlook in the future without more in-depth work. Nevertheless, similar to when working with other clients, I had to accept the limits of my intervention.

As is shown in all these stories, understanding the *family in the mind* is an effective tool that can help to make meaningful connections between our inner world and the way we perform and also struggle within our role in the work environment.

Leila was finally able to make some significant changes in her organization, thanks to the realization that her reverence for the deceased patriarchal leader was impairing her performance and also her organization. She didn't have the luxury of time – of waiting for another charismatic leader to appear; she had to initiate the changes herself. Shaking off the *patriarchal model* and taking up her responsibility more clearly wasn't easy, though it gave her new energy and demonstrated her inner strength and sound leadership approach.

Zuri learnt to manage her 'double-edged' refugee state of mind, the inner sense of loss, and displacement as well as her extreme pride in her achievements in a more balanced way, slowing down and listening more to the emotional climate of her team and work context.

And finally, Bill recovered some sense of agency and trust, despite his dysfunctional upbringing and lack of parental containment.

As these stories show, there are powerful experiences and underlying dynamics at play we can't escape, but we can learn to manage them better without feeling too overwhelmed or affected by them. The consultancy journey helped Leila, Zuri, and Bill to bring difficult feelings to the surface, revisit family dynamics and connect those experiences with their current challenges at work.

When they were able to make those connections, it was easier to develop a new narrative of their situation and take some significant steps to make some changes or reach important resolutions.

Despite their differences in personality, emotional intelligence, and role and work contexts, they were all able to engage constructively with the reflective space and the 'benign' third and finally move on.

In the following chapter I discuss the role of couples in family businesses – a very interesting area of exploration and intervention.

CHAPTER 2

Couples at Work

It has been fascinating to work with couples in family businesses, exploring their dynamics around authority and hierarchy, their feelings of rivalry and competition, as well as their desire for closeness and differentiation in the context of loving relationships. Ordinary dynamics become magnified in an environment where couples must constantly move between the private sphere and the business environment. Anxiety about hurting or undermining their partner may prevent them from having clarity about decisions and directions, and the desire to protect their relationship can delay or inhibit important conversations. The distinction between their roles in the business and in their private life is frequently blurred.

The pressure of running a company often takes over the private lives of couples, creating a constant tension between family and work demands. On the other hand, their shared passion for their project can be a significant glue in their relationship. It provides an extra edge, something generative and challenging they enjoy experiencing together. Not surprisingly, they are often ambivalent about letting go of their 'full immersion' approach and hesitant to engage with work in a more balanced way.

It is in the couple relationship where we invest the strongest transference – from our past and from unrealized and unwanted aspects of ourselves. Our partner becomes the recipient of our expectations and desires, as well as of difficulties generated outside the relationship.

Well-functioning couples develop a capacity to contain each other's passions, challenges, and anxieties – though the intimacy of the relationship can create an intensity that is not always easy to manage. Learning to share the physical space can be challenging – and even more so, sharing the *psychic space* inhabited by the thoughts, ideas, and emotions of our partner. Physical and mental spaces are intertwined and can be difficult to navigate at times, yet this shared experience can also be a source of pleasure and interest in each other. The tension between similarity and otherness also colours the relationships

DOI: 10.4324/9781003613961-5

of couples, the desire for 'fusion' with the partner as well as the pull to be different and separate from them. All these dynamics play out in the private domain as well as in the business sphere and have an impact on how couples are perceived by the members of the organization around them.

In the following examples, I describe the dynamics of three couples – owners of family businesses in different organizational contexts – who all share a genuine loyalty and love for each other, as well as a great passion for their enterprise. I discuss how they take up their leadership role and how their relationship with each other affects the organizational dynamics. They represent different dynamics in the way they relate to each other: passion, desire, and difficulty around inclusion; fear of differentiation; competition and idealization.

PASSION, ENVY AND FEELINGS OF EXCLUSION

Dominique and Louise got married three years ago. Finally, once their children from previous relationships had grown up, they had the opportunity to start a new work venture together. They both wanted to run their own business, after enjoying very successful careers in the commercial sector. Their shared passion for innovative food gave them the idea and motivation for setting up a catering business with 'an exotic twist'. They had the funds to invest, though the new enterprise presented some financial risks.

When I first met them, they were just at the start of this enterprise and were facing some initial challenges. The people they had employed were not up to speed, while one of their children had gate-crashed the enterprise and was expecting to be fully involved in the business. They were also encountering increasing bureaucratic obstacles. Despite their working long hours, the business was progressing quite slowly. Yet their passion for each other and for the enterprise was palpable.

The idea of starting their own catering business came about shortly after they got together. It became, as I described it to them, the baby they couldn't have at this stage of life. Their excitement for their project was infectious, though also overwhelming.

'I can't wait to wake up in the morning and sit at my desk next to Dominique – chatting about our project, exploring new ideas and making something new happen', Louise told me with a big smile.

You could understand how their children and staff would feel left out from the couple's intense close relationship and their dedication to the project. I began to realize how these feelings of exclusion and possibly envy for their relationship had slowed the business down. Despite the couple's doubts, Ella, Louise's daughter, had managed to join the company; she wanted to be included at all costs, even if she had limited skills to offer. On the other hand, the rest of the staff weren't pulling their weight and didn't seem to be on board.

I wondered if an envy of the couple's intense relationship was too much for others to bear. Similarly, the feelings of exclusion from their relationship and from their passion for the 'new baby' were very powerful and were affecting the team dynamics. As a reaction to her sense of exclusion, Ella had imposed her presence – possibly also on behalf of the other siblings – while the staff had withdrawn their initial enthusiasm for the enterprise. Ella's presence was tolerated by the couple, though she wasn't fully accepted by them as someone who could genuinely contribute to the development of the enterprise; while the team was seen as lacking initiative and too dependent on Louise and Dominique for ideas and to generate initiatives.

Louise and Dominique needed to shift this perception and find ways of engaging with their staff and daughter differently. They were both insightful and capable of reflecting on their behaviour. Following in-depth conversations with me and with each other, they started to behave much more inclusively towards the staff and learnt to tone down their approach. Though their ideas for the business were exciting and innovative, they needed to involve their team in the creative process, rather than overwhelm them with their ideas, energy, and passion. This 'over-fertile' couple had to learn to build a containing structure for the staff where they could feel like real partners in the enterprise, too.

After a few months, I could perceive a significant shift in the business: Dominique and Louise's approach had been too informal at the beginning, but now they had begun to realize the importance of introducing a few simple structures, a basic form of scaffolding for their start-up. As a result, people felt better held and listened to. The introduction of regular meetings with the whole team allowed staff to experience greater ownership of the business and of future developments in it.

There is always a tension, particularly in new ventures, between the desire for an organic approach to growth and the introduction of structures and systems. Bureaucracy is often seen as the enemy of generative and creative processes – as if structures would suffocate the development of innovative ideas. Dominique and Louise began to appreciate how the new scaffolding provided enough stability for the staff and facilitated the team's engagement with the enterprise. Their capacity to review their behaviour and learn to stand back was starting to pay off.

Envy and jealousy of the parents' relations – the 'Oedipal dynamic' – and rivalry for a new baby are inevitable dynamics in the family context. There is an existential threat brought about by the arrival of a new sibling that, in this example, is represented by the new business absorbing so much of the couple's attention and love. Parents need to learn to tolerate intrusive and negative reactions and find ways of helping the children to manage their feelings of envy and exclusion.

Dominique and Louise had been in too much of a hurry to launch their new venture without realizing the emotional and practical impact of their approach on the people around them. Marrying and starting a new business in middle age, they felt they didn't have the luxury of time.

Learning to engage with the emotional dynamics at play in their organization was key. It provided the foundation for introducing meaningful changes in their approach to the team and the whole enterprise. Only then were they able to take substantial steps forward to develop their dream venture.

In contrast, the couple described in the next example had to face their difficulties in accepting their differences as a positive and potentially generative element in their relationship.

STRUGGLING TO BE DIFFERENT

As mentioned, a key dynamic in couples is the anxiety about feeling separate from each other – it can be challenging to allow oneself and the other to be different. Exploring and accepting differences can be experienced as a threat. Past conflicting relationships with siblings and parents can play a part, too, making it more challenging to perceive difference as a strength and a resource.

Nikolaos and Daphne sit on the sofa whispering to each other. They are debating what to discuss in their session with me. As a couple, they convey something tender and intimate, as well as a desire to be perceived as a strong collaborative pair. They have both worked in social justice organizations for many years, though in different contexts. Finally, they have an opportunity to set up a significant project together, which they have called Rainbow. If successful, they are planning to create a new organization with a group of associates.

Rainbow aims, through training initiatives, to support disadvantaged groups in exercising their rights, accessing legal help, and becoming more involved in their local communities. It's an ambitious endeavour that requires the capacity to engage with multiple stakeholders. It is both exciting and anxiety-provoking.

Nikolaos and Daphne were aware from the start that they needed to learn how to work together; hence their request for me to accompany them on this journey. Nikolaos has a specific expertise in the subject of the project and quickly became the main point of reference for the stakeholders. While Daphne brought substantial experience in training and involvement with local communities, Nikolaos was more strategic and conceptual in his approach and had developed the methodology they were using as their central training tool. Despite some familiarity with the method, Daphne felt initially quite anxious and insecure, and referred to Nikolaos as the principal partner of the enterprise.

'I have never tried this methodology before, I'd rather Nikolaos takes the lead', she muttered.

I noticed how, at the beginning of our work together, she underplayed her skills and expertise, despite her many years of experience in the field and her perceptiveness about the dynamics and psychological aspects of the project. On the other hand, Nikolaos seemed at times too protective of his methodology and reluctant to look at the project from a broader perspective.

I observed how the emphasis was on their similarities as a couple, even in the way they dressed – they often wore similar outfits. There was an unconscious reluctance to engage with their differences from each other and an underlying anxiety about facing potential conflicts and disagreements. It seemed easier to accept a 'hierarchy' between them than to explore their different views and perceptions.

At the beginning of their second session, they told me – with some trepidation – they had had an argument. Nikolaos had been quite critical of Daphne about a report she had written. Daphne felt hurt, though she was very quick to accept Nikolaos's criticism. What they described didn't seem to me to be a major issue, though it was experienced and presented by them as such – such was their drive for harmony that any small disagreement became inflated in their minds.

We reflect together how challenging it was for them to disagree and how anxious they feel if they perceive the other as being emotionally distant.

Daphne and Nikolaos both came from complex family backgrounds and had experienced many personal challenges. It was very important for them to be perceived as a very cohesive and thoughtful couple. However, for me to be effective in their intervention, they needed to be able to engage with their differences, modelling a way of working that valued diverse views and perspectives.

Their close relation as a couple also provided a refuge from the pervasive turbulent and conflicting energies that exist in the field of social justice. Working in this field, where differences sit at the core, might have also enhanced their desire for sameness as a protection from the conflicts, confrontations, and challenges of that world. The roots of the way they related to each other were to some extent connected to family histories coloured by conflictual dynamics, but also to how they themselves represented 'the couple in their mind'– an island of sanity and respite in an environment polluted by disagreements and disruptive dynamics.

Part of my consultancy work was helping them to develop a belief that their differences, rather than being an obstacle, could produce a creative outcome. Though still very cohesive in their approach, something gradually shifted. Daphne became more assertive and open about expressing different views, and Nikolaos more tolerant of some criticism of his style and methodology. Having a 'benign third' (see Part 1) witnessing, and commenting on their dynamics, created a space between Daphne and Nikolaos that allowed them to have some distance from each other and to inhabit different perspectives without feeling too threatened by this.

SIBLING RIVALRY AND IDEALIZATION OF THE COUPLE

At the other extreme from Daphne and Nikolaos, Alice, and David, founders of Growth – a successful social enterprise – continually emphasize their differences and are openly quite competitive with each other. When we meet via Zoom, they always sit in different rooms, as if to underline their separateness. Our conversations are lively and intense, with colourful and direct language – maybe a reflection of their client base.

Ten years after they started it, Growth has developed significantly and is recognized as a beacon of good practice and innovation. It has supported many young people from very disadvantaged backgrounds through art and sports projects in local communities across the country. Alice and David, in their forties and full of energy, have also developed a high profile for themselves; particularly David, who is often invited to talk about their business model and their success stories in national and international settings.

Their rivalry is mainly amicable, though there is an edge at times, suggesting a tension around power and who is in charge. The dynamic of rivalry is mainly generative and allows for the exploration of different perspectives on the business. Alice often brings up controversial themes, and is more critical of the staff, while David, regarded as the founding father, has a softer and more tolerant approach. Their differences don't seem to inhibit their staff, who have learnt to engage with them in different ways. They tend to go to Alice for clarity on structures and processes and to consult David if they run into trouble. David is seen by everybody as the main leader of the enterprise, something that Alice accepts and resents at the same time.

The couple are very proud of what they have achieved and consider their approach to be quite unique. Underlying this feeling of pride for their enterprise, I can also sense an idealization of their relationship as a couple. I come to understand that the idealization is both a defence against the external world, which is often perceived as undermining and unhelpful, and an inspiration for continuing to be creative and transformative.

However, the idealization of the couple, though quite subtle, represents an obstacle for more in-depth exploration. It is territory that feels dangerous to get into, almost non-negotiable.

Their hubris, though possibly helpful in the initial phase of their venture, could become limiting at a later stage (see Chapter 3, on founders). The inability to question properly each other as business partners and the tendency to lean back on an idealized perspective of themselves could hinder the development of the organization and slow down potential innovations in it. I wondered if Alice and David's idealization of their coupledom was both a defence against the anxiety that their differences could create a split between them, and a protection against the possibility that Growth, despite being very successful, was more ordinary that they wanted to believe.

In their mind, Growth was unique, far superior to other social enterprises, thanks to their commitment, innovative thinking, and courage. Ordinary wasn't part of their vocabulary.

However, Alice and David eventually had to come to terms with the need to review their leadership approach and accept that the idealization of their coupledom was holding the organization back, making their staff too dependent on them for decisions, inspiration, and new initiatives. They realized they had to let go of the idea of Growth as their super gifted child and of themselves as the invincible couple, and to face instead the fact they were both special and ordinary.

The dynamics of couples at work is relatively uncharted territory, though a very interesting area to explore. The couples I have described were married and working in family businesses. However, there are also 'professional couples' that, though not romantically attached, present similar dynamics: they can be very wrapped up in each other, idealize their relationship, and exclude others. The way they relate to each other can have a significant impact on their organizational context.

Understanding the dynamics at play and the influence of professional couples' approach on their teams and colleagues can also offer a perspective on what is projected onto them by the organization. Couples might be unconsciously driven by the team to behave in a certain way in order to protect them from fear of failure or anxiety of survival.

The idealized couple could act as a good antidote towards the feelings of helplessness against a crushing bureaucratic authority, as shown in the case of Growth, while the passionate couple can protect their team against feelings of failure and fear for their survival.

Helping couples to be aware of how they relate to each other can be transforming for them and, consequently, have a positive effect on the organization they lead or they are part of.

Having considered some of the challenges faced by couples who have built their own businesses, in the next chapter, I discuss the dynamics behind the role of founders, the 'proud parents' of new ventures, and start-ups.

CHAPTER 3

Founders

Proud or Narcissistic Parents?

After listening to the stories of several founders, I was struck by my own reactions. Though I was incredibly impressed by their achievements and drive, I felt at times annoyed by an element of grandiosity I detected in their perception of themselves and their enterprise. Their attitude seemed to represent a 'pioneer syndrome'– a mixture of pride and arrogance about the uniqueness of what they have achieved. This underlying dynamic was always present, though with different tones and subtleties. It reminded me of my experience with some parents of very gifted and successful children, and my sense of exasperation and maybe envy in relation to their immense sense of pride and desire to show them off – such as the exceptional child violinist and the future Premier League footballer, while my children didn't show any interest in music and mainly played sport for fun.

I wondered if a degree of narcissism is essential to help you believe in what you have created and protect it from the external world; it can work as a shield to safeguard the enterprise and your identity as founder. 'Healthy' elements of narcissism can possibly strengthen confidence in oneself and in the creative endeavour, though 'unhealthy' narcissism can derail the journey.

Narcissism – meaning to take oneself as a love object – is something we all have to some degree. In its pathological manifestation, it affects our capacity to be affected by other people. On the one hand, 'healthy selfishness' can offer some protection from disruptive dynamics and envious attacks; on the other hand, 'unhealthy selfishness' takes us to the territory of narcissism, where we wrap ourselves in the comfort blanket of our self-belief and self-rightness and we are unable to engage with the world around us.

Though none of the people I will be describing stepped into the realm of toxic narcissism, there had been moments where I felt they were close to crossing that boundary: specific situations when they were unable to engage with the different and critical voices around them, including mine.

This often happened when the internal and external pressures felt too unbearable – hence the 'narcissistic option' became very tempting.

DOI: 10.4324/9781003613961-6

When people are in this state of mind, they are unable to answer the question, *'How are other people right?'*, which means recognizing other people's points of view, even if they are significantly different from ours (Shapiro). It's a question that is very central to my work, as trying to answer this question helps us to understand other perspectives, even when we are totally convinced of the rightness of our own ideas and position.

THE PERFECT ARTISTIC VISION

Sophie, charming and friendly, shows me around her arts centre, Grotto, based in an old industrial building. I feel like a voyeur, entering the vanguard territory of the new generation, full of colourful sculptures and gigantic pictures. It all looks slightly chaotic and overwhelming, though very powerful. Sophie walks around the huge rooms with confidence and pride, explaining the background and the stories behind some of the main pieces. I can feel her enthusiasm and passion for this enterprise.

Grotto was founded by Sophie ten years ago to provide an arts venue for young and upcoming artists as well as art events for children and local residents. It also runs a very popular café, with plenty of fresh handmade food. The organization had finally recovered after Covid – artists are re-engaging in interesting projects and people are filling the space again.

Sophie had been hit hard by the pandemic, having to manage her staff's discontent, their feelings of idleness and isolation, and a very tight budget. She also felt her own creative stream was drying up, and she oscillated between a desire to run away and the feeling of being indispensable to the organization. She felt trapped and unhappy. Although she was burnt out and quite depressed, Sophie was still convinced of the relevance of her artistic venture and of the role she continued to play. It was impossible for her to see anyone else leading Grotto at this stage. The more she felt criticized, the more she felt indispensable to the enterprise.

Today, she says, 'The team has decided to hold a meeting where they plan, I am sure, to ask the board to choose another director. I couldn't sleep all night, thinking of what to do. I have now prepared a statement I want to read at the beginning of the meeting, where I will explain all the work I have done for Grotto, which wouldn't exist without me!'

Sophie looks exhausted. Despite her youth and good looks, she suddenly seems older, showing her anxiety about the meeting ahead and fearful of her potential fall from authority. On top of her demanding job, she has a young child who has just started school.

She reads her statement to me, which sounds very defensive; her language is excessively strong, and she doesn't convey any understanding of where the staff's criticism comes from. There is something very possessive in her approach to the organization, as if she were the only one who can understand its vision and plan its future.

We start to unwrap the different layers: the impact of Covid, the frustration of the staff after spending so many idle months at home, her own exhaustion, as well as her determination and ambition. During our conversation, Sophie begins to relax – together we are able to contextualize the disruptive dynamics within the organization and the criticism towards her. She begins to see that people needed a 'negative object' to get rid of their frustration and distress. Projecting their feelings of anger and impotence onto Sophie has provided some relief for the team, but it's made her feel hurt and unappreciated. Sophie takes the attack and criticism very personally.

'I can sense they are planning to get rid of me', she says with great animosity. 'They want someone different – they're desperate to start a new chapter without me'.

Gradually, she starts to appreciate that, inevitably, her director role attracts very powerful projections, emphasized by the feelings of distress and uncertainty her team had experienced during lockdown.

Projecting uncomfortable feelings onto others is a common dynamic in our personal and work relationships. This process can escalate in situations of great stress, creating an atmosphere of mistrust and splitting among the individuals involved, as Sophie had painfully experienced.

People in a leadership position are particularly subjected to critical and negative projections – it is almost an invisible clause in their job description and something leaders need to learn to tolerate and manage. 'Holding the centre' (Gould) is challenging; it means being resilient and to continue to provide containment under very difficult circumstances and relentless criticism.

Sophie comes from an artistic family who had a great belief in her abilities. After she lost her father when she was still a teenager, she became particularly driven, as if she needed to prove her worth. With Grotto, she made a significant mark in the artistic community – despite her young age and limited resources. Her pride in what she had achieved is understandable, though at times it prevents her from seeing other people's contributions and leadership potentials.

Over several sessions, Sophie starts to recognize the roots of her defensive response to her team's criticism, and she begins to relate to her staff in a more open and understanding way, giving people more responsibility and taking a step back. Her different approach, together with a new business impetus after the long inertia of the lockdown, produces a significant shift. The atmosphere is more relaxed and collaborative, and the team shows a renewed engagement and energy.

This example illustrates a fascinating interplay between the key traits of the individual leader and the organizational dynamics. Sophie's approach, rooted in her personal history, made her excessively proud of her own 'creation' and very protective of her own vision. Her personal attributes – drive, creativity, and 'positive narcissism' – which served her well at the start of the enterprise, were getting in the way of embracing a new stage of the organization and were exposing her limits as a leader.

There is always a connection between the personal characteristics of the leader and the organizational dynamics, as shown in all the examples in this chapter. The particular 'valency' of a leader – their specific traits, inclinations, and approach – are inevitably interwoven with the organizational undercurrents. Through our work together, Sophie started to disentangle these dynamics and understand the part she was playing in hindering the organizational progress and future.

In the situations that I will be looking at next, the tension between healthy and unhealthy narcissism takes different shapes, though there is a common thread that links all the stories, which shows the complex balance between vision and aspiration and the capacity to accept one's limits and one's need for others.

IDEALISM AND THE FEAR OF GREED

Martha, bright and entrepreneurial, founded Dot a few years ago, a boutique consultancy that operates in the third sector. A well-connected Oxbridge graduate, Martha had quite an easy start on the work front. She comes from a family of distinguished public servants and has breathed a sense of duty and service all her life. She feels strongly committed towards her community and society at large.

Dot is now well established and has gained a good reputation for the quality of its work and ethical principles. It is small – five partners and an office manager – with a flat hierarchy. The partners see themselves as a young, cool, and innovative group. Despite their popularity, their income is modest. There is a degree of nonchalance and embarrassment towards money, as if they fear to be defined by it. Though everyone is paid the same, there is a visible difference between the partners in many respects, including their public image, capacity to win new projects, and amount of time they work. They are also quite reluctant to charge their clients substantial fees, even when the clients can afford them. This position, though on the surface progressive and unselfish, creates a dynamic that could potentially have a negative impact on their business. The position of taking the moral high ground prevents them from acknowledging and engaging with the competition inside and outside their consultancy firm.

A position that takes the moral high ground – idealizing one's own goodness and attributing 'badness' elsewhere – can create a misleading context, where the idealized image of the enterprise can play down the importance of the business objectives. Dot's approach and flat hierarchy are beginning to reveal some cracks among the partners. Their initial sibling harmony is starting to wobble.

Martha comes to our meeting with the partners in a bad mood.

She seems particularly serious and quite cross, her usual friendliness gone. She looks around the room with a degree of hostility, as if she can barely tolerate to be here.

She says she has had an extremely busy week and has felt very alone in dealing with complex clients and new referrals. She is usually very positive and upbeat, but this time she is angry with her colleagues – in particular with Jon, who never brings in new work and does much fewer hours than her. Martha, charismatic and driven, is very well known in the non-profit sector and has generated many consultancy opportunities for Dot. Jon, though competent in a niche area, is a backstage person who lacks ambition and determination.

'Shall we talk about money, or is it a no-go area?' I ask.

They look uncomfortable, but somehow relieved. The spectre of greed – 'the deadly sin', and fear of contaminating the idealized vision of themselves – is momentarily put on hold.

Their lack of hierarchy and differentiation, which has shaped the start of their venture, seems out of date and unhelpful today. Dot has now reached an adult stage, but it is still stuck in adolescent dynamics. Their idealism and desire to do good have become a shield against the business demands and the need for an internal structure that fits the organization's new stage.

Talking about their differences – in talent, leadership capacity, and earning power – feels very challenging, as if changing their sibling configuration would undermine their fundamental values. It represents a narcissistic wound in relation to their aspiration of holding the high ground in a commercially driven environment. They have thrived in their belief that they are different – more generous and ethical – than many similar organizations. Commercial considerations have always been regarded as a potential threat to the internalized image of themselves and their organization.

Gradually, over many conversations, there is a visible shift in their position: the possibility of reviewing their roles and earnings becomes more real. They start making plans about a radical restructuring of their internal systems and salaries. Despite their difficult journey to reach this point, I can sense their relief in finally managing to move forward.

The risk of crossing the narcissistic bridge has been avoided. My voice, initially experienced as mainly critical, has been heard.

Pedro, a social entrepreneur, also struggles to be challenged about his position and perspective, as described in my following story.

PROUD OR ENTITLED?

We are sitting in Pedro's lovely office overlooking a vast, leafy park. It is there that Spes's clients engage in gardening, yoga sessions, and art initiatives. The building buzzes with activities and exudes energy and drive.

However, Pedro is not in good space: he looks enraged. He just heard, after months of battles with local and national authorities, that one of his pioneering projects has been blocked by a 'bunch of daft and out of touch bureaucrats who take pleasure in making my life difficult'.

Spes was built from nothing. Now well established and highly respected, it has been nominated for several awards. The organization's support structures and training for ex-prisoners have gained a lot of praise for their innovative approach and for diminishing the stigma of prison among many communities.

Pedro is incredibly proud of what they have achieved. An only child doted on by his parents, Pedro was an early developer: he did everything in a hurry as he couldn't wait to jump to the next venture. This attitude was a fertile background for his entrepreneurial aspirations and gave him the confidence to pioneer something new and radical. He is a winner and doesn't take to loss easily.

Though I understand the origins of Pedro's anger and frustration, I feel increasingly uneasy. There is an underlying sense of entitlement that permeates his conversation; as if, given the success of his enterprise, he shouldn't be challenged or questioned. He is convinced his organization has the right approach for this project, and nobody else in the country is remotely able to gain similar results with such a demanding client group. Though I believe in Pedro's capacity as a leader and in his innovative vision, I can also see how his organization still needs to develop and how challenging he finds giving other people the authority to lead.

Like Sophie and Martha, Pedro feels an extreme attachment to the enterprise, which represents almost an extension of himself. His rage and frustration signal his difficulty in recognizing his limited power and influence and his ambivalence in having to depend on others for the success of his organization.

While pride can be a healthy expression of self-worth and confidence, the result of a secure internal base, it can, in contrast, be a manifestation of arrogance and superiority – possible evidence of a narcissistic state of mind.

Pedro's 'healthy narcissism', so crucial in Spes's success – the enthusiasm, positivity, and vision that had inspired so many – seems relegated to the past. He is locked in an 'I am right' position that exacerbates his differences with others and could become a major obstacle for Spes's development and growth.

Reluctantly, Pedro listens to my feedback on what 'I heard': the arrogant tone of his response to the bureaucratic system, the undercurrent feeling of entitlement colouring his argument, and his defensiveness in relation to any criticism of his organization. This isn't an easy conversation – reflecting on his own behaviour feels painful. The shadow of potential failure and shame colours our conversation.

'You didn't fail, one of your projects failed', I comment.

Finally, we are back in the 'consultancy space' – our place for reflection and review – which he has avoided until now, being too focussed on and concerned about his battles with the external world.

Pedro's reaction seems connected to an omnipotent image of himself. Omnipotence, on the positive side, can provide a sense of agency, hopefulness, and confidence; it is a key ingredient in the creation of an enterprise – without omnipotence human achievements would be curtailed. On the other hand, full-blown omnipotence can have very disruptive outcomes.

Pedro, successful and confident, struggles to accept real and potential failures and reconcile the image of himself and his organization with loss and a slower pace. The 'golden child' seems lost in a world that doesn't often reward innovative and creative thinking and doesn't look too bothered by mediocrity and lack of vision.

Pedro's reflective journey involves learning how to manage his disappointment without losing his positive omnipotence, which is still a great asset for his organization.

Sophie, Martha and Pedro have all been able to grasp significant learnings about themselves as innovative entrepreneurs and to look at their 'shadow side' – at the elements of arrogance, entitlement, and omnipotence that have coloured their leading role. Through their journeys, despite painful and uncomfortable discoveries, they have found a renewed awareness and energy to embrace the next stage of their ventures.

In the next chapter, similar themes are explored in the complex context of family businesses, with their constant tension between the family system and the business system.

CHAPTER 4

Family Businesses

It's been fascinating to work with family businesses, entering that familiar territory of intimacy and warmth, as well as witnessing profound disagreements, rivalry, and fights for power. Being allowed into someone else's family and feeling included, even with a degree of ambivalence, is very seductive. I've felt at times quite the voyeur when observing another family's dynamics with all its complexities, challenges, and strong emotions. Their entrepreneurial side and their creativity, as well as capacity for innovation and forward-thinking, have occasionally given rise to a mixture of admiration, envy, and competitiveness in me. I've wondered at times why I haven't been bolder and more courageous in my own career or risked a new venture myself.

Learning how to manage such conflicting feelings is part of my trade, though I find family businesses particularly challenging, as they inevitably touch on primary emotions: I can easily identify and empathize with what is going on within my clients' family or feel critical of their behaviour with their siblings, parents, or children. In fact, there's a 'business' side to every family. The way we manage the household – such as the family finances and the running of the house – intertwines with our family dynamics and it's frequently a setting in which we experience and project frustration, disappointment, or rivalry.

In family-run businesses, family dynamics are often played out in the actual business domain, creating a confusing experience in which it can be difficult to take up professional roles or feel fully authorized to lead and make business decisions. A particular example that springs to mind concerns a father and daughter whose company I once worked with.

'Delta has bought you your new car, a well-deserved reward for your commitment to the company', I remember Phil saying with a broad smile to his daughter. As Delta's chief executive officer (CEO), Phil had approved a bonus for Helen – knowing she was struggling financially, and she desperately needed a new car. A nice gesture, though to the outsider (myself) it seemed

DOI: 10.4324/9781003613961-7

quite confusing. Did Helen deserve the bonus? Or was it just a gift from a loving father disguised as a reward for her commitment to the company?

In my private conversations with Phil, he had often expressed doubts about his daughter's capacity to lead and take on more responsibility. Helen was hardworking and very loyal to the firm, but lacked the entrepreneurial talents of her father. Was the bonus a reparative gesture for her father's mixed feelings about her performance?

In this incident, as elsewhere, the focus of my interventions was on helping my clients to separate the 'family' system from the 'business' system and learn how to manage the interface between the two, without being drawn into mixing their professional roles with their family roles. It's usually a tough journey that requires discipline and determination, as blurring family and business can be experienced as the more comfortable easy option. Avoiding muddling up the personal and professional is one of the main challenges in family businesses – a behaviour and a habit people struggle to give up. Marking the territory between the two systems, acknowledging the role they are in when discussing an issue, and protecting the family sphere from too much contamination from the business are daily struggles.

In this chapter, I describe how different family businesses have dealt with old patterns, new challenges, and the desire to change and grow. My first story considers the complexity of succession in a family of landowners.

LEAVING THE OLD WORLD BEHIND

It's a beautiful autumn day and Tabitha is driving me through her sprawling estate. I'm struck by the size and beauty of the grounds and sit quietly while she tells me about the history of the place and shows me recent developments – the farm shop and the extensive vineyard.

'You're quiet... What are you thinking?' she asks me. 'Doesn't Bellpark look amazing?'

I can sense her pride about the long history of her family's ownership of the land and the innovations she and her husband have introduced.

However, it's been a torturous and challenging journey for Tabitha, as it was for Tristan, whom we met in Part 1. Her father, though very fond of his daughter, never trusted her to take over the estate. He was hoping her first husband could eventually run the business, but he wasn't interested. Tabitha went on to develop a career as a designer in Paris and came to the estate mainly for holidays and family occasions. Then her divorce coincided with her father's declining health, and she started to spend more time there. She began to develop some ideas about how to improve the enterprise, make it more profitable and better aligned with a changing world.

Despite this, her father continued to hold on to his position and became increasingly controlling, as he could sense his daughter's renewed interest in the estate and her desire for innovation. It was an extremely frustrating time for Tabitha, who felt very conflicted between her affection for her father and her resentment at being stuck in a powerless position. This situation lasted a few years, until her father's death.

She got in touch with me a year after her father passed away. Though she was now in charge of the estate and had already implemented several interesting initiatives with her new husband, she was increasingly aware of her difficulties around coming to terms with what had taken place before. While technically in charge as the lawful heir, she knew her father hadn't trusted her to manage the estate, and only his death had made him surrender control of it to her. She was experiencing strong feelings of guilt, resentment, and anxiety about the future. Though her husband was very supportive and proving to be an astute business partner, she often felt insecure – as if the ghost of her father, in Mozart's *Don Giovanni* fashion, were present in her thoughts and reproaching her.

Grieving represents a conflict between different drives – preserving what is important and valuable from the past and re-establishing meaningful patterns of relationships where the loss is accepted (Marris, 1993). It's much more difficult to deal with the death of a loved one if we've experienced ambivalent feelings towards them. The grieving process becomes more complicated and takes more time.

Tabitha was struggling to separate the genuine love for her father from her bitterness for the leader of the enterprise who had excluded her for so long, giving her only marginal roles. The intersection between the two emotional experiences made the situation particularly unbearable.

Gradually, through revisiting old incidents and sharing her current concerns with me, Tabitha started to be able to separate out the two roles – that of daughter and that of business partner – and understand her father's position in the context of his own upbringing, status, and related prejudices. As an old-fashioned landlord, her father couldn't conceive the idea that a woman would have the ability and competence to run such vast and complex estate. He also hadn't fully worked through his disappointment of not having had a male heir who would have perpetuated his name and lineage. Tabitha also acknowledged her part in making the situation worse by bombarding her father with ideas and potential projects without trying to engage with him at a speed he could manage.

As a result of our work together, Tabitha was able to recognize the complexity of the situation in a more objective way – the history and tradition of her family and the role she'd played in her response to her father's approach to the business. She felt more at peace with the situation and started to feel grateful for the great opportunity she now had to use her creativity and drive to develop the estate in ways that were more in tune with a changing world.

While Tabitha had to learn how to accept her authority in her new role as the CEO of an old and well-established country estate, members of Blue Mer were struggling to legitimize themselves as a 'real' organization.

A FAMILY OF FRIENDS

There is a lively atmosphere in the meeting room, with people chatting in small groups and sipping coffee. They talk about their families, the last film they've seen, and there's the occasional remark about the political situation. A sense of warmth and camaraderie permeates the room. Their enjoinment of each other's company is palpable.

It has been an important morning that, hopefully, will mark the beginning of a new phase – an almost symbolic transition from the adolescence to adulthood of the organization. Blue Mer's members have finally realized they have to take some radical steps if they want their organization to survive and grow.

The organization was founded by a group of young social workers who were inspired by their charismatic mentor and teacher. Their central idea was to offer interventions at low cost within disadvantaged urban communities. Fresh from their training and full of creative ideas, they had approached the whole venture very idealistically. Now, ten years on, they have realized their original approach isn't sustainable. Many of them have young families and need a steady income, while Blue Mer, though still innovative and quite successful in its approach, doesn't provide enough financial stability for its members. There isn't a clear business model, nor has there been much forward-thinking about the organization's direction and vision.

Yet they are all deeply attached to an organization that gave them a professional identity early on in their career and a group to belong to. Their investment in the 'sentient' group – privileging feelings, loyalties, and values over task or performance – is palpable. They enjoy each other's company, discussing ideas, and feeling part of something meaningful. However, the 'sentient' mode has become a defence against developing the organization in ways to meet the future with a sound business structure in place that could create more projects and generate a real income for its members.

They see me as their godmother, friendly and supportive, so I struggle to be more challenging towards them, trying to convey difficult feedback with warmth and empathy. I can see my younger self in them, a mixture of idealism and naivety, with a vague sense of what is required for developing a well-functioning business. I need to be careful not to collude with their ambivalence around changing gear…

In their consultancy sessions with me, they gradually began to recognize their ambivalence in making their work more commercially orientated – almost as if they had to hold on to this selfless image of themselves as the only professional identity they could inhabit. Their approach had echoed the dynamics of Dot, the consultancy group described earlier. Now, they started to realize that developing different types of interventions, targeting wider sectors of society, and partnering with other organizations would give them a stronger base, without having to let go of their work with disadvantaged communities. But they had to relinquish the idealized image of their roles, a psychological position that had protected them from the complexities of a less linear trajectory and from the challenge of navigating an uncertain and contradictory work environment. This change also required them to pay more attention to bureaucratic systems, clarify their different roles and responsibilities, and make them more accountable for their work.

It is a first step in the right direction, though I am left wondering if they'll have the courage and the determination to change direction and pursue this ambitious plan – eventually replacing their 'family of friends' with a more mature professional family.

In a similar fashion, Kleos, the organization described next, also had to face significant upgrading and changes to their structures and processes, having finally realized that they were at serious risk of extinction.

A PROFESSIONAL FAMILY

There was an old-fashioned feeling about Kleos, both charming and concerning. Meeting the members in their beautiful old building, an imposing villa with a magnificent garden on the outskirts of a big city, took you back to the days of its founders and their pioneering ideas in relation to holistic treatments and alternative medicine; yet there was also a sense of detachment from the contemporary world, with its rapid changes of context, language, and technology.

Kleos, an association of medics practising alternative medicine, had existed for many decades, providing a professional home to generations of 'alternative' doctors. It was highly regarded for its training and scientific events, attracting many professionals, both nationally and internationally, from different fields and schools of thought. However, the depth of their training and their innovative approaches to health weren't matched by a robust organizational structure. Kleo's scaffolding was quite light and unstable: people worked very independently, without a clear system of accountability or firm boundaries.

A sense of membership had nevertheless developed throughout the organization, within which there were many levels of professionals who had trained together and been taught by the older generations. It was a tight circle of colleagues and friends. Its hierarchical structure – both explicit and implicit – had a strong impact on the organizational dynamics. The most senior figures were often experienced as untouchable and beyond scrutiny. This created a fertile ground for incestuous dynamics and 'family secrets'. On a number of occasions, people had turned a blind eye to the breach of boundaries or poor practice, particularly if a senior member was involved.

The association was behaving like a dysfunctional family, with secrets and confusion around boundaries, and, consequently, members were losing their sense of direction and experiencing a growing mistrust in each other. Good practice and the rich and interesting training activities were contaminated by an increasing lack of confidence in the association itself and the fear that it wouldn't be able to survive. The organization had mainly relied on its 'family/friends' system and had neglected the development of a robust business system, including addressing the association's lack of steady income and its growing expenses.

My work with the association focussed on both their resistance to engage with the business system, strongly connected with the dominance of the clinical over the bureaucratic side, and the toxic 'family' dynamics at play that had allowed the organization to slip and lose its focus and sense of direction. There was also an element of arrogance, connected to the association's distinguished history, which, in people's minds, placed the organization 'above' ordinary dynamics – a widespread perception that Kleos was capable of looking after itself without much input from outside.

Appointing me at this time of crisis was evidence of the members' willingness and desire to turn a page and make some substantial changes. Sharing their difficulties with an outsider and accepting her help marked a significant step.

As mentioned, Kleos had become a closed system where 'family and friends' roles' prevaricated or obfuscated professional roles. As a consequence, people tended to protect their mentors or close colleagues from scrutiny or confrontation about their practice, relinquishing their professional roles and responsibilities. It was often a subtle dynamic, though strong enough to pollute the association's sense of its own ethical integrity.

My intervention aimed at breaking that closed circle and inward-looking approach, encouraging members and leadership to take a different perspective and engage in structural changes that would provide stronger boundaries and clarity of task and purpose. The members gradually realized they had to take some radical steps if they wanted to survive. As was the case for Leila, the director of the social enterprise we met earlier, change was the only option. They started to introduce more robust structures of accountability, appointed people with business and finance experience to relevant committees, and created a more open system, inviting the input of experienced colleagues from other organizations.

These crises happened at a time when alternative medicine had become more mainstream. Kleo's long monopoly of the field, its history, and reputation had become less relevant in the context of several younger, cooler, and more agile organizations. They finally realized that without making some radical changes, they could easily disappear in a few years' time. As in other cases, it is what's happening in the external environment that ultimately creates the energy and drive for transformation.

Turning a blind eye to the breaking of boundaries and bad practice had been an expression of their difficulties in coming to terms with the idea that their association was more 'ordinary' than they thought – and subject to abuses of power and dysfunctional dynamics in the same ways as less enlightened or distinguished organizations. Coming to terms with being quite 'ordinary' marked the beginning of some significant and meaningful changes.

In contrast to this and my previous example, Grit has put business centre stage, as described next.

THE BUSINESS AS FAMILY

'My parents have always put business first; our company has been their shared passion, having created it from scratch, despite many hurdles and challenges. Grit is a great success – it's the "child" they're most proud of,' says Mira with a mixture of resentment and irony.

Grit, an innovative IT company, had developed fast, quickly gaining strong recognition in its sector. It was driven by a formidable couple, who, like many immigrant families, had a great determination to succeed and fit in. However, their three children, all involved in the company in different roles, didn't work well together, neither in the family system nor in the business set-up. It was their unhappy and dysfunctional relationship that had prompted them to look for help. They were also facing a crucial time concerning their ageing parents and the need to develop a succession plan. Their difficult relationships made facing succession particularly challenging: they felt rivalrous and resentful towards each other, though underneath this they were all longing for their siblings' recognition and affection.

They had spent most of their childhoods apart, having been sent to boarding school from a young age and then going to university abroad. Their parents, though caring for their children, seemed very focussed on their children's capacity to contribute to the enterprise and often expressed their disappointment in their abilities and performance. There was a sense of emotional neglect, as a result of the parents' exclusion of the children from their relationship with each other and for privileging the company over them.

Their father's strong attachment to the business and his prioritizing of business success over family probably represented an unconscious desire for his own father's approval, after he decided to leave his country of origin, never to return. He'd created a business to demonstrate his worth, skills, and resilience.

Grit was run in a paternalistic way, looking after its workforce with great care, who remained loyal to the company over the years. For the siblings, the company represented the unwanted third in their relationship with their parents, as well as the precious object they had grown to love and feel proud of.

The siblings' relationship with me was initially suspicious, and it remained quite ambivalent until the end. It was hard for them to put their trust in an outsider or to feel they could be dependent on a parental figure, given their difficult relationship with their real parents. Yet despite their ambivalence we made good progress. They realized that, in contrast to their parents, I was mainly focussed on them, trying to facilitate a better way of them relating to each other both in the business and in the family domain.

Telling me their stories about how they perceived themselves and each other created a shared canvas. They were moved by this experience – tearful, angry, and surprised… but also relieved to be able to share their experience with each other and be listened to. They realized their perceptions of their family history were quite different: they held different families in their minds. This realization created a shift in their understanding of their different positions within the family, allowing for more compassion and less animosity towards each other. It was a significant step that also affected the business system, generating more collaboration and less rivalry.

'We still have a lot to do,' said Mira, 'but the journey has started, and everybody seems to be on board.'

Eventually, the appointment of someone external – a managing director who wasn't a family member and represented a 'third party' within the business – created a new space and an opportunity for the siblings to regroup. They were able to find a work mode less loaded with family dynamics. This gave them a new impetus to engage in the next phase together and confront some of their difficulties with more courage and hope.

The organizations I have described all share a tension between the two systems of family and business. This tension remains the greatest challenge for family businesses – finding a balance between the emotional investment in the family system and the need to develop a sound enterprise, sufficiently distinct from the family's needs and dynamics.

Some contamination between the two systems is inevitable. The skill lies in learning how to manage the interface between the two systems and become aware of when there is too much unbalance or interference from the family domain.

Notoriously, family businesses struggle to be open to outsiders and as a consultant, it's difficult at times to gain their trust. The relationship is often coloured by suspicious feelings or a sense of threat from people who aren't blood relatives or part of their close circle – even when their own family dynamics are very difficult. After all, better the devil you know…

To return to the organization I mentioned right at the start of this chapter, I have been in conversation with Phil and Fiona, Delta's owners, for several years about finding a managing director for their social enterprise. They are both approaching retirement age and have many different projects outside Delta they're keen to develop, and the organization seems ready for a change. However, I keep feeling their resistance, though subtly disguised. They are reluctant to let go of their full authority and control over the company, despite their fatigue and desire to invest their time in other ventures.

They feel at a loss, as they don't have an obvious successor in the family, and are afraid of giving their 'baby' away, after so much investment and love. In this respect, their response to the issue of succession is not unusual and is characteristic of the experiences of many leaders who struggle to identify a successor, though it is usually a much more acute and tormented process for family businesses (see Chapter 5 on succession). As shown in the examples in this chapter, it's often the real threat to survival that finally mobilizes people to face and overcome their resistance to change and move forward.

The dynamic of succession, partly discussed in the vignettes above, is the focus of the next chapter.

CHAPTER 5

The Dynamic of Succession[1]

The approaching death of a parent can deeply impact family dynamics. In Shakespeare's *King Lear*, an ageing monarch, who is determined to stage his own succession, sees his overbearing demands provoke ambition, greed, and profound unhappiness, which lead to the disintegration of his family. Successions in organizations can be equally complex, triggering very primitive emotions.

Organizations don't usually pay enough attention to the dynamics of succession and to the powerful feelings affecting the experience of the people involved. The departing leader can feel pushed out and unwanted. The staff left behind may feel abandoned, experiencing the loss of protection and guidance. The incoming leader can fear people's judgement and comparisons and struggle to prove his or her difference and value.

These primitive emotions can remain unconscious and unacknowledged. As a consequence, feelings can get displaced or acted out into disruptive dynamics, leading to difficult and painful succession processes.

An example of a troubled succession occurred at the National Theatre when it was led by the great actor and director Laurence Olivier. Here, the succession process was conducted opaquely; actively managed behind Olivier's back, with his appointed successor, Peter Hall, sworn to secrecy. Olivier, who had no role in his heir's selection, was confronted with a fait accompli, and felt that he had not only been excluded but stitched up (Billington, 2013).

This example provides a glimpse into the difficulties of facing the end of an era. It underlines the guilt associated with letting go of a leader, particularly one like Olivier, one of the most distinguished actors of our times. This complex emotional context creates the conditions for 'acting out', exemplified by the stealth of Olivier's ostracism from the succession process. The secrecy of the succession process is evidence of the anxiety around confronting Olivier's likely disappointment and anger, and shows apprehension relating to embracing fully the need for change in the National Theatre.

DOI: 10.4324/9781003613961-8

The desire to take a parent's place is a very powerful dynamic. The guilt associated with the desire to take the parent's or leader's place is one of the central motives for painful and messy succession processes. The need to 'kill' the father is, as the psychoanalyst Winnicott says, an inevitable stage for adolescents to gain maturity and independence. Though it can also provoke profound guilt, as the following example demonstrates.

TU, BRUTUS, FILIUS MEUS....

A group of senior clinical directors of an acute health trust were under a lot of pressure. They had just come out of the pandemic and were now facing new challenges. Their staff were exhausted, and the chief executive officer (CEO) wanted to implement major structural changes. The current medical director was leaving; they were hoping for a fresh start with a new leader who could provide a containing presence in this turbulent context.

Luke, a senior doctor within their hospital, was asked to become the interim leader. He didn't have a good reputation: people thought he had a divisive approach and lacked empathy.

The directors were hoping it was just a transitional arrangement. However, the board and the CEO had a strong preference to recruit someone from inside the organization and felt Luke represented a quicker solution and a safe pair of hands. In this interim period, his shortfalls became much more apparent: he missed important details and was brisk and demanding with staff.

During a gap between two consultancy sessions, the directors decided to oppose Luke's appointment as medical director. It was a bold but necessary step. Their concern was genuine, and they had evidence to prove it.

When we eventually met, they told me they had been successful in preventing Luke's appointment. However, there was an uneasy and anxious atmosphere – no expression of triumph or satisfaction. Their sense of guilt about their action was obvious: as I pointed out, they felt they had killed their 'professional father'. It was difficult to bear their feelings of betraying a member of their own tribe, even if they knew they had done the right thing. It took them a while to accept emotionally that it was a legitimate action which would eventually allow the organization to choose a more suitable candidate and avoid future disruptive dynamics.

Killing off Luke, though challenging, didn't match the trauma of the following example.

Rejection and Ejection

What happened with Ravi was one of the most dramatic successions I have experienced. It was a real ejection of a leader who had been revered and worshipped, though also experienced as very dominant and even cruel. A culture of *omertà* (a code of silence and secrets within criminal organizations), due to the shared history of marginalization of most members of the organization, allowed the situation to escalate to a point of no return. People didn't dare to challenge him; he was seen as the champion of their cause and the main architect of the success of their organization.

Kiln, an international think tank focussed on education in developing countries, had attracted a diverse workforce with complex personal history and cultural background. Innovative and radical in their approach, they have developed a beacon of good practice on how to operate in difficult and challenging environments.

Ravi's fall from grace happened very fast, and Chia, who eventually took over his role, had been originally his protégée and most vocal supporter. There was a growing criticism that quite suddenly became a coup.

I could see how Ravi had brought some of the attacks on himself. His rather arrogant and autocratic approach, his contempt for many colleagues, as well as his success and charisma, made him a likely target for attack.

Nevertheless, such a difficult ending could have been avoided if Chia and other members of the executive team had taken a more constructive role in managing the succession. However, I could also sense how Chia, maybe not fully consciously, would see the benefit of 'killing the father' instead of engaging in a lengthy and complex succession process.

Also, their task and context had changed; the organization had become more mainstream. It required a different leadership style, with a more empathic and open approach. There was no need for a 'fight' leader anymore.

The executive team and the board, who allowed Ravi to become an 'autocratic father', couldn't manage a more thoughtful succession process. They had to reject and eject a leader who had become or been perceived as 'damaged goods'.

The following story describes instead the challenge of letting go of a team which has become the founder's tribe and professional family.

Tribal Dynamics

Tara is the founder of a pioneering department in blood diseases in a large NHS trust. She has been at the core of its development and success. After many years as a principal consultant, she was promoted to the trust directorate, a role she accepted with some ambivalence, as she has always seen herself as an outsider, irrespective of her achievements and success within her department.

Despite her new commitments and challenges, Tara still spends time in the department, clearly not feeling settled in her new role. She often goes back there on Wednesdays, the day her successor is not in. Though she doesn't sit at the same desk, she is still based in her old office. Unsurprisingly, people consult her when she is there; they feel reassured by her experience and wisdom. Yet, there is a widespread feeling she is keeping an eye on Dan, the new principal consultant – and not always in a benign way. Dan feels mixed and slightly confused towards Tara: as his mentor for many years, her advice has been invaluable. Now, he feels implicitly criticized and even undermined in his authority.

It wasn't surprising that Tara found leaving the department challenging; it has been her professional home for a great part of her career. Her identity has been intrinsically linked with her role within the department, being perceived as 'the mother of the team', but her continued involvement risks perpetuating a closed system and holding back the organization's development.

I was also aware of her ambivalence towards the leadership of the Trust: she often referred to them as 'the old school network'. As a woman of colour, it has not been easy for her to take a place at the top table, regardless of her competence and skills. However, she was highly regarded within the department, seen as a very capable leader and ultimately the team's matriarch.

The department was her *tribe*. Moving out of her tribe, even for a more senior role, felt hard. A few years away from retirement, it made sense for her to take up a higher position in the organization. A last chance to exercise some influence on a larger scale. Though, she wasn't ready. Her desire, emotional involvement, and passion were still in her old job: as a clinician and leader, she belonged there. Outside that tribe, she felt quite lost and foreign.

I have been reflecting on how leaving our professional tribe or allowing someone new to join our tribe can be tough. It can challenge our sense of identity and belonging.

The notion of an organization as a tribe can be linked with the organizational concept of closed systems: a system reluctant to be open and encouraging towards new members. One of the key dilemmas in this framework is understanding when the tribe is a 'force for good' – wanting to preserve the integrity of its approach and practice – and when tribal dynamics become an excuse for protecting one's own interests, position, and affiliations.

An extreme example of an organizational closed system is seen in organized crime syndicates such as the mafia. Given their nefarious intentions and brutal outcomes, the mafia can be understood as a 'perverse tribe'. Although originally, it wasn't like this. The mafia was born in Sicily as a way of life: an instrument to protect one's family from the injustice of imposed government.

The perverse state of mind, as described by Susan Long, 'is not simply a deviation from normative reality. It has to do with individual pleasure at the expense of a more general good. It reflects a state of primary narcissism'.

Key aspects of 'perverse tribal dynamics', such as nepotism or protecting our tribe at all costs, can cast a shadow over any process of succession.

For example, it may prevent people from challenging a leader who has stayed in their position for too long, or who is blocking new people or diverse actors from joining the organization. These dynamics also impact new leaders from taking up their role effectively if they are perceived as outsiders, or too different from the dominant culture. They can be marginalized and undermined in their authority.

Behind this defensive attitude and protectionism is the anxiety of losing our own tribal identity if the status quo is challenged or changed. When we are part of a tribe, it can become very difficult to leave. We might feel anxious about letting go of our professional home and network, fearing to be excluded from our 'sentience' group, where we invest our loyalties and feelings, and lose the status and comfort of belonging to a particular group. There is often the concern of not having another tribe to go to.

If our own professional identity is too strongly related to our tribal identity, leaving might feel almost impossible – as Tara's example shows. Her ongoing presence in the department enables elements of perverse tribal dynamics that help maintain a closed system and inhibit the embrace of new approaches and fresh leadership.

While the nature of work has dramatically changed in the last 20 years, it remains a crucial element of our identity and emotional investment. A lack of work or disengagement with our role and our organizational environment can lead to emotional withdrawal and low self-esteem and diminish our capacity to engage with the external world beyond our immediate circle of family and friends.

An important ingredient for a successful succession is the desire for the next chapter, a libidinal investment in a new venture. It is also key to moving forward without feeling a sense of betrayal towards the tribe we are leaving.

It is our need for belonging that drives us to be part of a group that shares values and purpose. Yet, this shouldn't mean our professional tribe has to be a closed system. An organization can't survive as a closed system. It needs new blood and injections of different ideas through new generations and to explore diverse approaches. The organization also needs to maintain its core practice, providing a sense of stability and continuity. The tension between innovation and continuity, openness, and stability is difficult to sustain, particularly if our own professional identity is strongly associated with our tribal group.

I have experienced and witnessed the challenge of succession – letting go and letting in – in my own professional world. The transference towards a particular individual in a role can be hard to shift. The new person stepping in – the 'step-parent' – can be a source of anxiety, suspicion, or contempt. This tribal dynamic becomes even more acute in family businesses, where the complexity of family dynamics plays a huge part in how succession is handled, as shown by examples described in other chapters.

Stepping down from a role in an organization doesn't always have to be final. The departing leader can still offer some significant contribution if the role generates from a real organizational need, rather than from the desire to placate or appease. However, in Tara's case, by not letting go, she risks replicating King Lear's domineering presence in the succession process and reinforcing the closed loop of tribal dynamics.

Some of the issues explored above are strongly connected with the following chapter on siblings. The themes of belonging and tribe are also very relevant to siblings' sense of identity and relationship with each other, and parental figures.

NOTE

1 This chapter draws on 'The challenge of succession: leadership dynamics and conflicts in different contexts' in Work Matters (Cardona, F. Routledge, 2020) and 'Tribal Dynamics in succession' (Psychodynamic Practice, 2021).

CHAPTER 6

Siblings at Work

Our siblings are both our first allies and our first competitors. Through them, we learn how to work with other people, how to negotiate, compete and compromise. Siblings can provide friendship, companionship, and love, as well as be the source of rivalry and envy. They are woven into the same family narrative and keep each other in mind at times of happiness and sadness. Our relationships with our siblings are often the longest in our lives – coming before friendships and life partners – and could also be highly developmental, as we 'experiment' through them how to relate to others.

Inevitably, our early experiences with our brothers and sisters colour the way we engage with our 'work siblings' – our peer colleagues or co-leaders sharing the same work context. With the latter, we can project feelings and expectations, as well as repeat family patterns and dysfunctional relationships. In family businesses, working with real siblings can be particularly challenging, creating confusion between the family roles and the business roles and activating dynamics that belong to the domestic domain.

The first stories I share here are about 'work siblings', people who aren't actually related but share a sibling dynamic, while the last vignette is about biological siblings in the context of a family business.

In this chapter, I will also discuss how the 'siblings in the mind', the internalization of our sibling relationships in our original family, can affect 'our role identity' – our perception of ourselves in a role in the workplace – and how the impact of the premature death of a biological sibling can play out in a professional context, generating feelings such as guilt or an excessive sense of responsibility.

I try to convey the powerful influence, often unconscious, that our experience with our siblings, our birth order and the position we took in our original family can have on how we inhabit our professional role and relate with colleagues and partners.

My first example is about two work siblings, the founders of a successful start-up.

DOI: 10.4324/9781003613961-9

SIBLINGS, PARTNERS AND UNACKNOWLEDGED DIFFERENCES

Sitting on the sofa in front of me, Hamish and Leona are in deep conversation with each other, almost unaware of my presence, as if they just need a space and a witness to help them reflect together. I am impressed: they are young, bright, full of ideas and already quite successful.

Their energy and creative stance are infectious, and I am immediately drawn to them. The way they juggle the competing demands of family and work reminds me of my younger self, while their ages, interests and challenges resonate with the experiences of my own children. I am conscious of the traps of identifying too closely with my clients (see 'The Benign Third', page 7); still, I struggle to keep time boundaries, swept up by their intensity and creative energy.

The two young co-founders of Jade have developed an events company with a 'heart': they are determined to make a strong social impact. They have been upfront from the beginning about their ethical stance and choose their clients carefully – always working with organizations in challenging and controversial areas.

They want some help to move into the next stage of their organization and to work on their own relationship as co-leaders, aware their backgrounds in psychology and art don't equip them for dealing with the challenges of leadership; and the difficulties they face have also put some strain on their friendship.

Hamish and Leona started their company in their mid-thirties and now, ten years later, are well established in their niche area. They are both very driven, highly creative and determined to make a mark, while raising their own young households. They both come from broken families and are keen to create a cohesive and harmonious professional family. But at what cost?

They avoid being open with each other about their disagreements over priorities, approach to the staff and long-term goals. Though there is a genuine emotional connection between them, and a true interest in their different perspectives, they find it difficult to be critical of each other's decisions and practices. Their desire to keep things smooth and friendly connects to their anxiety about potential conflicts and splits – something they seem to want to avoid at all costs. Their fear 'to differ' is also projected onto their staff group, still with a flat hierarchy, and they struggle to confront underperforming team members.

Through a 'shared environment' in early life, siblings can develop a strong bond that softens conflicts and differences. Their shared understanding of their world can promote positive relations with one another in their adult life. However, siblings (the word originally meaning 'brotherly love, familial affection') can be similar, yet also very different. In a business context, the dynamic between their similarities, connected to the 'shared environment', and differences – of approach, perspective, and skills – if worked through, can become a source of strength and creativity.

For 'work siblings' Hamish and Leona, their shared environment is the company they have created together, something they are proud of, though still feeling quite apprehensive about its future. Their anxiety about the sustainability of their business, combined with their own personal vulnerability around issues of conflict and difference, makes them very 'protective' of their similarities and reluctant to address their differences with one another.

Together, we start to unpack this dynamic and see how their 'repressed' differences can be an obstacle to the healthy growth of their enterprise. They can see how their family backgrounds of painful separations impair their capacity to disagree and differ, and have influenced the organization's DNA, creating an environment prone to avoiding conflicts and confrontation.

'You were brilliant in our last pitch, so clear and passionate. We wouldn't have won this project without your great presentation', Hamish says now to Leona.

Their criticism of each other is always preceded by several compliments about each other's talents and skills – the anxiety about damaging their relationship is a constant shadow.

It is difficult to stay in that zone, although with firm encouragement, they are able to discuss some of their disappointments and frustrations and realize they can do this without falling out with each other – an important step forward that marks a shift in their partnership.

Leona and Hamish now meet regularly – they are starting to address not just their business's priorities, but their different points of view and disagreements with each other. This shift is beginning to make an impact on the company, and they feel their relationship is more robust as work siblings.

In contrast, conflict and difference are at the core of the relationship of the co-directors in the following example.

ELDER SIBLING LEADERSHIP

Lucy and James, co-directors of a social enterprise, are regularly at loggerheads. Lucy, in particular, is often critical of James's laid-back approach and lack of decisiveness.

'I can't believe you let him off the hook again, after so many warnings', she says to James now about one of their colleagues. 'They will never take us seriously if we never discipline anyone!'

Lucy and James seem stuck in two contrasting positions – the older 'professional brother' who is quite distant and aloof, and the impulsive and strong-headed younger 'professional sister'. They have adopted these roles in the work context almost as if they were real biological siblings.

Their social enterprise – a cooperative – is, by definition, an organization with a flat hierarchy. Asserting their authority as co-leaders is extremely difficult in this context. People work very independently and often refuse to follow or avoid following instructions coming from the centre. Lucy and James' challenge is to take up the role of joint 'elder siblings' without slipping into a parental role that would be unacceptable in an organizational culture which is focussed on equality, and which is ideologically against hierarchy.

It seems a paradoxical position: implicitly, they should act as 'parents' to create a sense of containment for an organization with complex clients and very limited financial recourses; explicitly, they need to act as elder siblings, available and actively helping to deal with the complex bureaucracy and constant crises, though without any real power over their team. Lucy and James' different positions and constant arguing are a response to the pressure of roles with a lot of responsibility and very little authority, both inside and outside their organization.

I try to encourage them to 'upgrade' their elder sibling roles – developing a clearer picture of what they can and need to do – without upsetting the delicate balance of a peer culture where marked differences and a pecking order can't be tolerated. My initial idea of creating a mini 'constitution' to spell out their key principles is welcomed at first, but later abandoned, and the possibility of considering sanctions if directives are not followed is experienced as anathema. James, especially, is very anxious about appearing too 'authoritarian' and parental in his approach. I feel increasingly frustrated and disappointed that all my efforts to make them more effective and authoritative come to nothing. I start to realize that their 'elder sibling' role is, practically and psychologically, very constraining. They can try to influence, nudge and encourage, but they can never instruct nor sanction, as parental figures would do.

Siblings do not form a concept central in psychoanalysis: Freud thought sibling relationships were characterized by primitive hatred and hostility. Similarly, in organizations, the focus is often on the hierarchical vertical paradigm, rather than on lateral leadership or relationships, and there isn't a template for lateral leadership as such, or, if there is, it is still quite tentative. The model in the mind tends to be the vertical paradigm – it is still difficult to engage with a more horizontal framework. Though there is always a hierarchy between older and younger siblings, the lateral element is dominant in contrast to the vertical position of parental roles. The challenge is learning to recognize its difference – a more cooperative and interdependent leadership approach – rather than interpret it as a lightweight version of the parental model. It is also related to the task: a sibling leadership could be very effective in certain environments.

Reviewing my work with Lucy and James, I came to understand I had to start from the assumption that elder siblings couldn't take the parents' place, particularly in this organization, and to recognize their position as 'elder sibling' leaders without trying to emulate a parental model of leadership. My initial frustration with them was partly related to my own reluctance to let go of the parental leadership model that represented much more familiar territory for me. The challenge for me as a consultant was learning how to help them to influence and develop their organization from a lateral position, identifying opportunities that a sibling leadership can generate and grow and a language that could convey a more collaborative and horizontal approach.

In the example that follows, I examine the impact of 'the sibling in the mind' on the development of professional identity and feelings of self-authorization and value.

THE 'INVISIBLE' SIBLING

Roy, an experienced IT consultant, still sees himself as a late developer and struggles with issues of confidence and self-authorization. He talks, with humility, of many interesting projects he has developed and contributed to, as if he shouldn't own the success and results achieved. His tone of voice, posture and language lack the authority you would expect from someone with his experience and skills.

A recent health scare prompted him to get in touch with me. Though he has a busy schedule, he doesn't overwork, and his work–life balance seems fairly good for a man in his late forties. I wonder what lies beneath his current stressful situation and we start to explore his career and professional development in the context of his life.

While revisiting his early years, a significant event comes to light: the loss of his younger brother after a very prolonged and painful illness.

'It is particularly poignant year for me... Jack was only eight then,' he says, and explains how this year marks the tenth anniversary of his brother's death. Roy describes movingly how, while still very young, he supported his parents and, after his brother's death, had to deal with their grief as well as his own. Gradually, Roy's conflicting feelings start to emerge: on the one hand, the 'survivor guilt' – he was the lucky one who was spared and survived; and, on the other hand, the feelings of pressure around having to 'be successful' enough for both of them.

The survivor is a victim as well as the person who has died. The death of someone close, predictably, has an impact on how the 'survivor' develops his or her own identity and is often coloured by an underlying feeling of guilt at being alive and well. When a sibling is seriously ill or dies, conscious and unconscious jealousy and rivalry seem to become true – the aggressive phantasies seem powerful enough to become real. The loss of a sibling could also mean losing the parents the child has known, overwhelmed by their own grief and struggling to relate to the surviving child.

At an unconscious level, the 'absent' brother had never left Roy. His guilt and sense of responsibility to 'do well' for both of them have kept his brother 'alive' and have interfered with his own sense of worth and full ownership of his achievements.

'It's a burden and a responsibility that's so difficult to shake off', he explains.

Our exploration of these difficult feelings helps Roy to connect his current stress with the anniversary of his brother's death – a possible trigger for his health scare.

In the following sessions, we discuss how he could start to let go of some of his guilt and feelings of responsibility, give himself permission to enjoy his professional successes, and take credit for his achievements without the shadow of his brother. It is a challenging journey that Roy now seems ready to engage in – being proud of what he has been able to build, without feeling compelled to apologize for the person he has become.

While Roy grapples with the shadow of his brother 'in the mind', the next example describes an unusual sibling relationship, where 'siblings in the mind' have also played a part in the dynamic.

AN UNEVEN SIBLING PARTNERSHIP

Georgia and Hans are an unlikely pair. Georgia, smartly dressed and tall, with a crown of silver hair, has a commanding presence, while Hans, shorter and dressed in a casual outfit, looks uncomfortable in the limelight. Although very different in age, experience and background, they have set up a company together. They are the founders of Ark, a consultancy with a focus on health and well-being in the workplace.

The decision to form a partnership was precipitated by Hans's redundancy and by Georgia's advancing years and desire for a 'third act'. Georgia had been a consultant for Hans's previous organization: she was impressed by his sharp mind and big ideas. Hans liked Georgia's in-depth approach, rigor and openness towards younger generations. The idea of a partnership started to take shape.

The 'unthought known' was their difference in experience, status and perspective. Their differences were left dormant in their subconscious — never fully explicitly acknowledged. Their time frame was also different: Georgia, in her late sixties, was in a hurry to get something started, as she didn't have much time in front of her; whereas Hans had a young family and struggled to be fully focussed. Their relationship became tense, partly the result of their difficulties in recognizing their different stages of life, experience and seniority.

Hans had a complex relationship with his family; he felt disappointed in and quite distant towards his siblings, particularly his older brother. He desperately wanted to show Georgia he was her peer and didn't want to look up to her. Georgia started to have doubts about Hans's potential as a leader, though she felt guilty about her ambivalent feelings, which contradicted her perception of herself as open-minded and generous towards the young. The eldest of five, she had been very close to her youngest sisters, a template for the relationship she developed with her own children and other relationships at work. Georgia was now regretting her decision to start a company with Hans and felt she could do much better on her own.

Through our conversations, they painfully began to address the difficulties in their relationship with each other and to make some links to the 'siblings in the mind' that informed the way they related to each other. Their initial blindness to their differences was also evidence of their difficulty in acknowledging their contrasting personal situations: Georgia's sense of urgency around creating something exciting and challenging – a grand finale at the end of her career – and Hans's feelings of overwhelm and anxiety, trying to balance his energy and emotional investment between his younger family and the birth of a new organization.

Hans eventually accepted a less central role: he realized that even in sibling relationships there can be a hierarchy, without this necessarily meaning that he had to give up his personal authority or the hierarchy limiting his capacity to make a substantial contribution to the enterprise. Becoming a 'junior partner' gave him permission to spend more time with his family and enjoy more flexibility, while Georgia was able to exercise her full authority and experience without needing to apologize or make herself smaller than she was.

My last example is based on a family business, where the complexity of moving between the family system and the business system has created strong tensions and distress among the siblings.

COMPETING FOR PARENTAL LOVE

Joe and Melanie, looking edgy and apprehensive, started to argue from the start. In our initial session, they didn't waste any time in bringing up old grievances, accusations of disloyalty and strong criticisms of each other. I felt quite overwhelmed by their animosity, anger, and pain.

Their parents had founded an organic products company, a pioneering initiative ahead of its time. It was now a very successful enterprise and aiming to move from a niche market to the mainstream. The two siblings have been involved in the company from an early age and have very limited experience of working in other organizations. This was the only world they knew.

Their ageing parents, too preoccupied with the development of the company, had neglected the succession process and found themselves now without a clear plan. Joe, the eldest, was conscious of the increasing conflicts with Melanie and decided to ask for help.

It became clear, almost from the beginning, that the battle between them wasn't just about their roles and power within the company – it was very much about being recognized and valued by their parents. It was a fight for 'parental love'. The company had become the battleground for getting their parents' attention.

Their parents had struggled to manage their double role as company founders and parents. Their focus on the enterprise, 'their third child', had taken up a huge practical and emotional space at the expense of their own family. Now older and quite frail, they couldn't fully engage in a succession plan, while each of their grown-up children wanted to claim their own 'position' in relation to their parents and to feel seen and acknowledged. It all felt too late.

Joe and Melanie needed to find a way to work with each other and move from 'parental leadership' to 'sibling leadership', reclaiming some authority and power in relation to their parents, as well as recognizing each other's competence and roles in the company.

Our journey together focussed both on their private roles within the family and their work roles within the company. Together, we revisited painful episodes of their childhood as well as conflicts and disagreements in the work context.

Growing up within the company didn't give them the autonomy and authority that a proper separation from their parents could have brought about. They had never really left home and tended to look at the world of work through the lenses of their own company history and dynamics. However, revisiting their shared environment, their different experiences and perspectives created the opportunity to develop some trust in each other. My presence, focus, and benign 'parental' role allowed them to express their frustration and disappointment with each other without feeling too threatened and overwhelmed by their feelings. There was something quite ordinary in their rivalry and disagreements that I regularly underlined, though this was often complicated by their dual role as siblings and business partners. They also realized that investing in each other could, in part, compensate for the lack of parental attention they had experienced growing up. Joe and Melanie also knew they didn't have a choice if they wanted to repair their relationship as well as engage in a constructive succession process.

Siblings are important 'internal objects' – the psychoanalytic concept that our inner world is inhabited by mental representations linked to our early experience with significant people. They can provide continuity, companionship and love and be a reference point for their shared family history. Learning to manage their competition with each other, as well as acknowledging their differences, is key to building both a healthy sibling relationship and effective lateral leadership.

In an increasingly changing and turbulent world, sibling leadership roles, when properly developed and thought through, could be as effective and containing as parental leadership roles and also provide a more agile response to the current fluidity of organizational contexts. However, people might feel more vulnerable or exposed without the 'protection', even if illusory, of more vertical hierarchical structures. Lateral leadership is psychologically challenging: it requires us to accept accountability for our decisions and actions, while demolishing expectations placed on those authority figures previously regarded as our main sources of guidance and containment (Haffington, 2004). That said, 'sibling leadership' – a horizontal, less hierarchical and potentially more collaborative approach – could be an effective template for leadership in new ventures and start-ups, creating an environment that encourages the staff to take up their own authority, rather than relying too much on their leaders.

This distribution of power and authority is an important factor in every relationship, not just between siblings. The following chapter addresses the difficulties and challenges of abusive organizational dynamics.

CHAPTER 7

Abusive Organizational Families

I haven't encountered many abusive organizations, but I have listened to the stories of several individuals who have experienced or observed abusive dynamics in their workplace. The abuse has been mainly related to the breaking down of fundamental boundaries, creating a climate of anxiety and a lack of trust. As a result, people have developed a dysfunctional or disordered attachment to their organization or leadership, feeling often displaced, unsettled and emotionally lost.

The concept of a secure attachment, so central in the development of a child, can also be applied to the work domain. Without an attachment to a meaningful activity, we can feel disengaged and unfulfilled. Abusive dynamics can contaminate our relationship with work, our trust in the organization and the confidence in our ability to be effective and creative.

The dynamics I describe in the following pages have often been quite subtle, yet they have had a powerful impact on the teams and individuals concerned. My examples, though presenting different degrees of toxicity and disturbance, are all permeated by feelings of powerlessness and confusion – the effect of the stress and anxiety people have experienced.

The central focus of the consultancy has been in helping my clients to recognize and face the abusive dynamics at play in their organization, resist the temptation to turn a blind eye, and learn to regain some sense of agency and choice.

As the next story illustrates, sometimes it takes a dramatic event to finally face the reality of abusive organizational dynamics.

A CLOSED SYSTEM

'On paper it looked all good', says Harry in a tense voice, looking anxious and lost. 'I liked the college'. I very much wanted the role of head of counselling;

DOI: 10.4324/9781003613961-10

I was keen to start this new venture. I knew of previous problems with some members of staff – one teacher suspended, one investigated – but I was unprepared for the magnitude of the issue. When I first arrived at the college nobody knew I was coming, the headmistress wasn't there – I had no office.

> In the first week I had to start a disciplinary with several members of staff who slept in the staff room after the end of the year celebration and were drunk in front of the students .... My role should have been to help and train the staff against possible allegations from the students; instead, it became safeguarding the students against their teachers.

Since joining the college Harry had become increasingly anxious. Then, a few months into his role, despite being quite young and fit, he had a stroke. That incident prompted him to seek some help to address his situation. What emerged from our initial conversations was a picture of a closed organizational system – an organization unable to set clear boundaries, and which had carried on in the same unbounded fashion for many years.

The previous head, Ralf, had to leave when he was discovered to be having an affair with one of the teachers who was married to another member of staff. Jane, an external candidate, was subsequently appointed in his role. Staff and students loved Ralf and didn't like Jane very much; they made her life quite difficult. The revelation of the affair didn't seem to have any major impact on the collective attitude to rules and boundaries, despite the growing concerns of the college's board of governors. The staff were so entrenched in their own world that they failed to appreciate the severity of the situation they were in.

Harry thought the new head was nice, but he didn't trust her judgement. A recent incident related to the appointment of a teacher. Harry had reservations because of some doubts about the teacher's capacity to manage boundaries. He felt the school couldn't afford to employ someone with that record. However, Jane went ahead regardless.

I had a sense of an organization dominated by 'incestuous' dynamics, where boundaries were regularly broken, almost without people realizing they were doing it – as if the college, too wrapped up in its own internal dynamics, wasn't properly open to and engaged with the external world. Though this environment didn't seem to have a particular negative impact on the students, some members of staff were greatly affected by the broken boundaries and the lack of a serious plan to tackle the organizational dysfunction.

Harry was thinking of leaving, but he was worried how it would look, having recently resigned from his previous job. 'When I'll apply for another job, people will realize I have left two jobs in two years', he said. He also had a strong sense of duty; he was determined to help the college address some of its key problems and develop frameworks and policies that could prevent similar incidents from occurring in the future.

Yet the impact on his health was worrying and I felt the pressure of encouraging him to leave as soon as possible. I unusually found myself giving advice quite early on in our coaching relationship, being very alarmed by the situation. The college didn't seem like a safe place.

I also felt as though I was in a safeguarding role in relation to Harry. His stroke was significant evidence of something wrong in his working environment and he didn't appear to have the emotional resilience for such a demanding and stressful role. There was the additional risk to his own reputation – being tainted by what had gone on before in the college. So, quite early in our work together, I said, 'I think you should leave...' However, it took the whole academic year and many coaching sessions for Harry to finally quit his job!

Differently from the traumatic events described above, the following story shows the impact of more subtle, yet nevertheless powerful, abusive dynamics.

THE 'ORIGINAL SIN'

I still have a vivid memory of my lunch with Pierre, the director of Spark, an organization caring for people addicted to drugs and alcohol and sponsored by the Church. The organization was impressive, with plenty of activities and interesting initiatives – it had a good rate of success, quite unusual in the addiction field. Pierre was a very dynamic and entrepreneurial leader who came from a different sector and had turned the organization around.

During our lunch, a member of staff, Catherine, came to talk to Pierre about an urgent issue. Pierre, in a casual and quite dismissive way, referred to her past experience as a Spark's client, saying, 'I remember how lost and confused you were...'

When she left, he filled me in with more detail about her troubled personal history: 'Catherine came from a highly dysfunctional family – an alcoholic father and a weak and submissive mother; it's no surprise she ended up here!'

I was very disturbed by this incident and felt increasingly uneasy. I didn't need or want to know all of that. Though I was aware that several staff members were former clients of the organization, a common practice in many enterprises dealing with addiction, I felt something had been violated: the fundamental right of someone to keep their personal history confidential and to be treated as a professional rather as an ex-client. I later linked this incident to the religious belief of original sin – the sin that should always be with us – and to an organizational culture that encouraged dependency, but also a form of surrender.

Stark's leadership actively promoted a dependency on the organization as part of moving their clients away from their dependency on drugs. As a result, their clients developed a strong transference towards the organization that allowed many of them to move on and give up their addiction. They shifted from a highly damaging form of dependency to a healthier dependency on an organization that cared for them and gave them tools to regain some normality in their lives.

Though this approach made sense and was positively constructive, it also demanded a degree of submission that I found disquieting – as if the clients/staff had lost their right to be separate from the organization and their entitlement to put their past behind them without being regularly reminded of their previous 'sins'. The subtly abusive nature of this relationship, while often unconscious, created an element of toxicity in the whole system. The religious imprint of the organization, though providing inspiration, dedication and care, also encouraged an unhealthy culture of surrender that limited the development and choices of its staff.

This consultancy project happened many years ago. I was unable to confront this dynamic then, due to my limited experience as a consultant and my feelings of overwhelm in relation to Spark's approach – a distant echo from my childhood religious experience and a poignant reminder of my ambivalence towards and criticism of some of its practices. Still, many years on, this incident has stayed with me and has informed my understanding of similar abusive dynamics in other contexts. I feel now more able to spot them and, hopefully, a bit braver in addressing them.

In similar situations, I would now 'listen' to my feelings of uneasiness and disquiet and would translate them into an intervention with my client – for example, by asking Pierre why he felt the need to share personal information about his staff member with me and to reflect with him on what the potential risks and damage might be of such an unbounded approach for the organization.

The following example relates to a more explicit breach of boundaries that had a profound effect on the morale and confidence of the team involved.

BREACH OF A PRIMARY BOUNDARY

Sharon, the director of a psychotherapy clinic for families and children, was in a state of great distress when she got in touch with me. One of their senior therapists had recently disclosed he was in a relationship with the mother of one of his young patients. Both married, they were going to separate from their partners and were planning to live together. Oscar, a very experienced and well-respected therapist, understood the seriousness of the situation, but remained unapologetic: 'We love each other', he simply said.

After an internal investigation, he was dismissed, and his licence to practise as a psychotherapist was also going to be revoked. His colleagues, some of whom were also personal friends, were stunned and profoundly hurt by this revelation; they felt compromised and tainted by what had happened.

'I went to a conference recently and felt uneasy about admitting where I worked, in case the rumour had spread', Sharon admitted now, clearly upset.

Oscar had broken the primary rule of the therapeutic relationship, and his colleagues felt betrayed by him. They also feared this incident could affect the clinic's reputation and potentially damage its future if patients and referrers became aware of what had happened. Trust had been broken in a business where trust was its main currency.

On the one hand, the team had to face their vulnerability as an organization and let go of an idealization of themselves as professionals incapable of wrongdoing, while on the other hand, they had to mourn the loss of their close colleague and work through their own feelings of anger, disbelief and sadness.

There were also questions in my mind about the organizational culture – how it could have contributed to this breach of boundaries. The clinic's approach reminded me of a common dynamic in family businesses: the confusion or overlap between the 'family system' – their friendship and comradery with each other, the many social occasions spent together, and the work system, with its professional boundaries and tasks (see Chapter 4 on family businesses).

Despite having a director, the approach of the clinic was very collegial, and the hierarchical structure was flat. The system of accountability wasn't particularly clear; people worked quite independently, trusting each other's judgement and professionalism. Supervision had been mainly provided from within, with the occasional visiting supervisor.

And, of course, the staff were inevitably affected and 'contaminated' by the complex family dynamics brought by their clients, often the result of broken boundaries and dysfunctional relationships.

Their organizational culture, familiar and friendly, might have contributed to them turning a blind eye to something that was happening under their nose. In that context, Oscar felt also unable to disclose, at an early stage, what was happening to him emotionally, at a time when alternative outcomes might have still been possible, or the emotional turmoil could have been worked through in a much more thoughtful and less dramatic way.

As a result of this painful incident, the team started to discuss how they operated and to address the risk posed by having unclear structures and poor accountability. The structure of the team was reviewed and changed: they created a leadership team with distinctive responsibilities and introduced a more robust system of supervision as well as clearer policies about professional conduct.

The organization now realized that, like many of the families they treated, they had neglected to build strong boundaries around their team or create proper structural systems to support their challenging work.

As often happens, the team was mirroring some of the dynamics brought to them by their clients – a phenomenon I have called "sponge effect" to describe the way a team can absorb and soak up the central dynamic operating within its client group. In this case, the team's constant exposure to dysfunctional situations had increased their risk of being unconsciously contaminated by their clients' dynamics.

The illusion of being in some way superior to ordinary organizations – different and special – had been shattered, as well as the omnipotent phantasy they could do no wrong, thanks to their training, dedication, and ethical principles.

From an organization that wasn't critical enough of itself, we move, in the following example, to an organization dominated by a leader who was highly critical of the staff he led.

ABUSIVE UNDERCURRENTS

Bolton was a successful organization that had campaigned in the field of human rights very effectively. Thanks to its director, Hao, the organization was now well established, highly respected and starting to be known internationally. Bolton's approach, workshops, and interventions were recognized as examples of outstanding practice and innovative thinking. The organization had the support of several corporate institutions that often purchased Bolton's services for their own staff.

Hao came from the commercial world. Passionate about the field of human rights (heightened by his own personal history as the son of political refugees who had fled their country and lived for many years in fear of being sent back), he wanted to bring some of the ethos, efficiency and focus of the business sector to the world of non-profit organizations. In this respect, there were many battles for him to fight, internally and externally, in a context that worked very differently and lacked the entrepreneurial edge and commercial acumen Hao felt were necessary to stand out and be relevant.

In the first three years of his leadership, he was able to introduce significant cultural changes and innovations with the support of the executive team he had recruited, though he kept the board at arm's length: he believed he had the expertise and leadership ability to turn the organization round without 'external interference'.

However, his high expectations and ambitions for himself and for the organization started to have an impact on his physical and mental health. It was at that point that I was asked to support the executive team. The board wanted Hao to take a step back and give more responsibilities to his senior team.

It wasn't easy. Hao had developed a centralized approach and struggled to delegate important tasks and decisions; but he had now no choice.

While working with him and his team, I gradually realized how quickly people could fall from grace and become the object of his criticism or sarcasm. Highly intelligent and a quick thinker, Hao couldn't tolerate slowness, mistakes, or a lack of effectiveness. Almost every time we met, he told me how someone had disappointed him.

I felt at times quite on edge with him, too, bracing myself for potential verbal punches. This only happened a couple of times, but it gave me a taste of what it must have been like for his staff.

I remember an incident at an away-day with the executive team and the board. When I arrived at the venue, I realized we would need an extra room for working in small groups. When I asked Hao if that would be possible, he responded in a sharp and loud voice, 'Yes, if we can deduct the cost from your fees'. I felt humiliated and disrespected, as if I were asking something extravagant, purely for my own benefit.

This type of behaviour became exacerbated by his increasing sense of losing power. In his individual meetings with me, he regularly slated his colleagues, communicating a sense of disdain and contempt for their performance and behaviour. Ironically, the only person he still rated highly was the one who eventually replaced him and didn't stand up for him when the board decided to sack him.

Under Hao's leadership, there was an undercurrent of fear and anxiety in the organization that prevented people from naming and addressing these damaging dynamics. My attempts to bring these undercurrents to the surface were regularly pushed back or ignored. The subtle abuse and bullying were tolerated because of Hao's success and the fear of damaging Bolton's prominent position and reputation. Paradoxically, the organization that championed human rights was unable to apply its principles to its own members – as if there was only one way of approaching their task and challenges: Hao's way!

In my conversations with Hao, I was also struck by his dismissive attitude towards his family of origin, as if he wanted to distance himself from them emotionally, showing an ambivalent attachment to his parents and siblings. I suspected his earlier successful career had come at a great cost. From an ethnic minority background, though privately educated in the British school system, he had probably been the subject of bullying himself and might have often been treated with contempt, something he let slip in one of our conversations. This experience might have been at the root of his increasingly abusive behaviour at a time of stress.

The organization was also going through an impasse and needed to refocus on new objectives and revisit its position in the wider environment. The uncertainty and lack of clarity about the organization's future contributed to the sense of instability experienced by the executive team and intensified Hao's critical stance.

The consultancy provided some opportunity for reflection and accompanied the transition to a more collective leadership. However, the abusive undercurrent remained mainly unexplored. It was finally dealt with by the abrupt decision of the board to dismiss Hao – in a hasty and quite brutal way. It was a decision that the executive team didn't resist or object to (see Chapter 5 on succession). Keeping the board at arm's length had compromised Hao's relationship with them and generated mistrust in his ability to lead the organization into the next phase.

I wondered if this traumatic ending could have been prevented if Hao and his team had been able to recognize and address some of the dynamics at play, rather than sweeping them under the carpet. This situation also mirrored the world of human rights, with its contrasts and challenges: highly idealistic and principled, though also polluted by the toxic and complex dynamics of the groups they were trying to help.

Like the psychotherapy clinic described earlier, this organization had soaked up some of the dynamics of the world they inhabited without being able to process and fully understand the impact this had on their practice and team relationships. Differently from the clinic, Bolton's executive team and Hao were too ambivalent towards the consultancy process to allow any in-depth exploration to take place. At a rational level, they wanted to address their situation, but at an emotional level, they couldn't go there, maybe too frightened to discover their fragility and potential capacity to abuse and exclude others.

The red thread that connects these stories is the result of some key strands they share. All the organizations were – though to different degrees – closed systems. In families, abuse often takes place when there are inadequate influences from and exchanges with the external environment – where there is little genuine interaction with the world outside the family and limited control from outside.

The organizations described in this chapter all showed some reluctance to engage fully with their community and wider environment. They had created their own kingdoms but lacked the oxygen from the outside world. They were also confusing social roles with professional roles. It became easy to slip into 'social' roles when their professional roles became too challenging. The abusive dynamics mainly occurred as a result of members of staff having broken significant boundaries and the organization itself lacking the scaffolding to support their staff with its complex tasks.

One of the key learnings from all the examples is the importance of paying attention to the emotional undercurrents and the early signs of dysfunctional and potentially disruptive dynamics. It is often the impulse to turn a blind eye – to avoid conflicts, upsets and confrontations – that allows the problem to escalate. Learning to detect early on the drive to collude and an avoidance of recognizing potential trouble is a fundamental skill – a muscle to develop and strengthen.

The consultancy with me, though with varied degrees of success, provided a space where these dynamics could be discussed and addressed. The realization of what was going on under the surface helped the people involved to regain some capacity to look at their work with a sense of perspective and to start to implement the necessary steps for organizational change.

In the next chapter, I discuss the impact of early losses on how people take up their roles in organizations and the significance of gaining an understanding of their effect on confidence, personal authority and the capacity to navigate organizational storms.

CHAPTER 8

The Scar of an Early Loss

Will I Ever Be Good Enough?

An early loss creates an emotional imprint on how we experience ourselves, engage with the world and develop relationships. It can give us resilience and courage, as well as make us more fragile and unsure of ourselves. The effect of an early loss often remains implicit in the workplace – kept hidden or barely acknowledged. It is something we tend to relegate to the personal sphere. The emphasis at work is on performance and effectiveness, and the wish to appear able and competent acts as a shield against making the connection with our early traumas or losses. Inevitably, the feelings provoked by early painful experiences, if not worked through, can have a strong impact on the way we inhabit our work role.

Listening to many professional stories has given me an insight into how an early loss can shape our approach to work and our capacity to navigate organizational storms, and how it can influence the way we take up a leadership role. In this chapter, I want to draw attention to a significant though invisible 'presence' in the work environment – an unhelpful shadow, when not recognized, for the individuals concerned. The focus of the stories is on my clients' emotional journey and the internal shifts that created the context for development and change.

In the following vignettes, I describe the impact of an early loss on the professional identity of three individuals – all quite different in terms of their family and cultural background, profession and class. They are linked by the premature loss of a member of their family and by the way this event has shaped their engagement with their career. They all have experienced profound self-doubt and strong feelings of not being 'good enough'.

All three approached me for coaching about issues concerning a lack of confidence and feelings of being stuck in their professional role. While the theme of an early loss wasn't the presenting problem, it came up in our conversations at a later stage.

DOI: 10.4324/9781003613961-11

In all three situations, coaching has been quite transformative, helping them to make sense of their experience in the work context and creating new connections between their personal background and the way they have inhabited their roles. It has also given them permission to let go of some of their guilt related to how they have dealt with their loss over the years.

They had all been ready to engage with this process; they were able to overcome their initial uncertainty and ambivalence to explore what had kept them psychologically and practically trapped in the past. This process required courage, openness and a willingness to trust me and the coaching process – something they all possessed. To accept someone else's help, we need to trust not only the other but also ourselves, recognizing the dependency and the reciprocity this entails.

Their significant early losses had cast a shadow over their work roles, often preventing the recognition of their achievements and potentials.

JASMINE, THE DE-ROOTED ADOLESCENT

Jasmine, petite and quietly spoken, is struggling to keep her business afloat. A talented interior designer, she has left a large firm to set up her own company. She has always aspired to be her own boss and a few years ago, she took the plunge. However, after a promising beginning, she now has very few projects. Many potential clients like her – she is personable, creative and shows genuine commitment to her projects – but eventually they choose to employ the services of someone else.

I wondered what lies behind Jasmine's inability to convince people she is the right person to hire: why she lacks the charisma, decisiveness and conviction to impress.

Jasmine also feels the pressure to make a real contribution to her family's finances. Her partner is the main breadwinner, and she feels ashamed that her in-laws are still providing financial support for them. She spends long hours at work without this translating into a substantial income.

I want to hear Jasmine's story to understand how some of the dynamics and events of her past are linked to her current difficulties. As I listen to her speak, two key events emerge: the sudden death of a younger sister and the family's move to her father's country of origin a year later. These events were clearly linked. The grieving parents wanted a fresh start for the family; they felt that moving home could be a way forward: they had the support of their extended family there and hoped the new surroundings could provide some comfort and fresh possibilities.

In her early teens, Jasmine suddenly had to leave her friends, school and the country where she was born. Her roots were severed – she felt lonely and isolated. It's no surprise she struggled at school and didn't want to continue her studies.

'I hung around with dodgy characters and spent endless hours in front of the computer. I had completely lost my motivation and drive', she admitted.

After a few years of small jobs and frustrating experiences, Jasmine took on a role with an NGO in Africa, in a challenging and quite dangerous environment. It was a significant learning experience and a major turning point for her. When she finally came back home, she decided to go to university. She was 26; her contemporaries had already graduated and were in professional jobs. She later moved back to England and continued her training there.

Listening to Jasmine, I felt profoundly impressed and moved by her capacity to overcome her difficulties and get to where she is now. To me, she was the opposite of a failure – she was someone with great resilience who, with quiet determination, had been able to rebuild her future.

I was also struck by the contrast between my own response and Jasmine's experience of feeling as if she were always left behind, constantly catching up – never quite where she wanted to be.

Revisiting and reflecting on her story with me gave Jasmine the opportunity to make new connections; for example, how the grief for her sister had dramatically slowed her down and how the guilt of being alive and well had played a part in sabotaging her own life. She also started to see the inner resilience she'd developed in her work in Africa that led her to pursue what she really wanted to do.

After a few sessions, Jasmine reported she was getting more work and she was gradually feeling less stuck. I also noticed how she looked livelier and more positive. The efforts she had put in looking to create new opportunities for herself had finally paid off.

I realized how gaining a deeper understanding of her emotional scars and connecting this with her current challenges was crucial in shifting her approach to work. I wondered if my reaction to her story – my appreciation of her resilience and capacity to move on – also played a part. As an empathic outsider, I was able to connect and name the different dynamics at play and refer to the relevant past, though strongly focussing on the present. My hope was to help Jasmine to shift from a 'loser' perspective – always behind, never where she wanted to be – to a 'winner' perspective, where she could take pride in her survival abilities and capacity to develop. Together, we created a new narrative (see Part 1).

Jasmine was emotionally ready to start that journey. Despite some initial ambivalence, she genuinely wanted to make some changes – she instinctively recognized that just working on 'external' elements such as strategy or presentation wasn't enough. She needed something internal to shift. Through the consultancy, she was able to see another side of herself: the resilient and capable woman who overcame her family trauma and the challenging experience of being uprooted to become a competent professional. Her late arrival in a profession wasn't an embarrassment or a symptom of her difficulties anymore.

It became evidence of her accumulated life experience, which could add depth to her work and role.

The following story focuses on a different response to early trauma with the additional complexity of coming from an immigrant family.

SAMUEL'S IMPOSTOR SYNDROME

Samuel felt stuck in his career. He couldn't see how to progress. Despite having successfully taken up senior roles – he had been a manager in a variety of organizations in the health sector – Samuel felt unfulfilled and constantly doubted his worth. He realized intuitively that some of his current dilemmas and uncertainties were related to his complex family history.

The eldest son of an immigrant family from an African country, he still felt over-responsible for his original family and elderly mother, much more than his younger siblings did. When the family moved to the United Kingdom, he was only two. A bright boy, he did well at school, but after his father's premature death he failed his A levels twice. This early failure continued to cast a shadow over the development of his career. In our conversations, Samuel often went back to this 'failure' as if he couldn't let it go – an 'original sin' that couldn't be erased.

The premature death of his father was a traumatic event for the whole family, but particularly for him. His modest background and the complexity of coming from an immigrant family strongly contributed to his sense of feeling like an 'impostor' in the organizational roles he was in. This powerful sense of not knowing where he belonged continued to colour his experience at work, despite a number of significant achievements and recognitions. I wondered what made it so difficult for him to acknowledge his achievements, despite his challenging beginning.

Listening to Samuel, I experienced a deep sense of heaviness – the heaviness passed on by his immigrant parents, by their expectations, frustrations, and difficulties. Failing his A levels became a symbol of having failed his father, who had struggled so hard to support his family. What he achieved later in his career never seemed to compensate for this 'original sin'.

'Maybe, now that you are fifty, it's time to forgive yourself', I commented.

The word 'forgive' provoked a flood of tears. He described how hard he had been on himself, trying to make up for the sacrifices his parents had made to bring him up. Yet I wondered if Samuel, as well as feeling guilty and inadequate, also felt angry about the early parental loss and, possibly, resentful at having to negotiate a new identity in a foreign country, as a result of his parents' life choices. Maybe these were the feelings that kept him stuck in the past, feelings that he struggled to reconcile with his sense of duty to his family. It was easier for Samuel to recognize feelings of guilt and sorrow than his anger and resentment about the events that had affected his life so profoundly.

The 'presenting' emotions of distress and insecurity often show just one side of the coin. In this situation, addressing what has been openly expressed is not enough. We need to pay attention to other communications under the surface, to the 'music behind the words' – engaging with another kind of communication, which is like grasping the main emotional dynamic behind a song or an opera in a language we don't know – and the undercurrents.

Through our work together, Samuel started to identify more clearly his mixed emotions and realized he needed to acknowledge them to be able to move forward. The sense of 'failure' that had haunted him for many years started to fade away, while a sense of agency and pride in his achievements began to emerge. Through my eyes, Samuel was able to see a different narrative, where the focus was much more on his capacity to overcome his complex family background, recognize significant successes and identify what he still needed to do to feel more settled and content in his role and career.

There are strong links between Samuel and Connor, my following example, with both coming from immigrant families and having a strong sense of duty and responsibility, determined to succeed despite their modest backgrounds.

CONNOR – THE DUTIFUL SON

Connor, the first member of his family to go to university, comes from a humble background: his grandparents were impoverished and uneducated farmers from Ireland. When his parents moved to London, they wanted their children to have the opportunities they never had.

Connor was bright and very good at school. He qualified as a maths teacher, which he became briefly before joining a tech company, where he started to develop an interesting career. Despite doing well, he grew increasingly aware of his inability to compete in a very driven environment.

'I am very reflective and tend to be quite cautious in my responses. This approach doesn't always work well in my work environment, where almost everybody drives on the fast lane', he told me.

While he appreciated being asked his opinion and included, he was never able to push forward his own agenda or requests. He was always ready to see the other person's point of view.

In our conversations we started to unravel what laid behind his compliant approach, which was starting to become increasingly unhelpful in such a competitive work environment. Connor's identification with the 'professional class' was quite weak, regardless of his achievements, appreciation from his peers and success in her projects. The huge leap of class – from that of his farmer grandparents to being a senior executive in a cutting-edge company – generated, often unconsciously, an uneasiness for him about his position and a pervasive lack of confidence.

I commented on how he also responded to me as a 'dutiful son' – always very appreciative and grateful for my observations and comments. It was at this point that Connor started to talk about his younger sister, who had died in his teens from a long-term illness. As a result of his sister's death, Connor suddenly became an only child, feeling the responsibility of carrying on his parents' expectations as well as supporting them in their grief. Now that he was in his late forties, the side effects of this family trauma and the impact of his social background were starting to emerge. Though he had had some therapy in the past, he had never made a conscious connection between the impact of his sister's death and his family's social background and how he behaved in a work setting. His earlier trauma and social situation were casting an invisible shadow over his work persona, holding him back and curtailing his potential.

Connor's increasing awareness of the underlying dynamics gave me permission to start challenging him on how he engaged with his organization and his colleagues – for example, I pointed out how easily he took a backstage position, always leaving the leading roles to others. As a result of our conversations, he started to see more clearly the role he took and gradually became more assertive in the work environment. It wasn't easy, as he had spent most of his adult life being accommodating: the dutiful son who took a reparative role towards his grieving parents.

As with Jasmine and Samuel, creating a new narrative was key to helping Connor perceive himself in a clearer light, allowing the shadows from the past to emerge. He was aware these shadows couldn't fade away – they were part of him. This process helped him to understand the inner challenges he faced and created the emotional context for developing a more confident approach to work. He could finally dare, from time to time, to take a leading role, without feeling guilty or inadequate.

These vignettes highlight the value of a consultancy/coaching space where it's possible to explore and link difficult and traumatic personal events to challenging situations at work. For Jasmine, Samuel, and Connor, coaching has been a tool for making significant internal shifts. The identification and discussion of practical changes are not enough by themselves. It is the awareness and the understanding of deeper dynamics behind the presenting issues, and the process of working through them and re-learning at a deep emotional level, which allows individuals to make lasting changes.

As a coach, listening to 'the music behind the words' has allowed me to facilitate the creation of a new narrative that includes events and experiences that have been left unexplored or avoided. However, this is not always possible. Sometimes, people find it too challenging to make these connections and avoid entering those territories; it can be too painful. They have a defensive armour they don't want to let go of. On the contrary, Jasmine, Samuel, and Connor knew that something wasn't working for them and were open to 'letting me in' and sharing their difficulties and distress. Together, we created a shared context for understanding and searching for meaning.

I also wondered if the context of the pandemic and lockdown had somehow accelerated the desire of these individuals to make some significant changes and had increased their capacity to be more open to change and transformation.

Vulnerability is often seen as something to hide or a quality to be ashamed of. The widespread culture of 'performativity' in organizations creates a climate where it is difficult to show our own difficulties to colleagues, employers and even to ourselves. The emphasis is often on results and performance rather than on belonging, loyalty and the ability to be open.

The capacity of the individual to address their early scars more openly is key to making the workplace more humane and conducive to bringing the whole of ourselves to our task and role.

The stories in the following chapter are about the absence of a deep family bond and its impact on their adult selves.

CHAPTER 9

The Absent Family

For some people, the experience of family relates to a sense of absence of a deeper bond – a lack of a containing environment in which we can feel understood and supported in our growth and development. The lack of such a containing environment in our early life can have a profound impact on our adult selves and our inner world.

In this chapter, although involving different personalities and situations, the stories all show the impact of an early emotional absence on my clients' professional personas: how their experience of absence has shaped the way they have inhabited their roles. The 'family' absence could be psychological, physical, or both, the result of inevitable circumstances or an implicit choice. Whatever form it takes, the experience of a significant lack of care, focus, and love has marked the way people have responded to the workplace and its challenges.

Julienne, my first example, had to grow up very quickly. Her parents were only partially available to her, being too preoccupied with their own lives and their failing marriage.

PREMATURELY ADULT

'I've been independent from an early age, since my teenage years. My parents were there, but also not there', says Julienne, a senior financial adviser at PDC, a large accountancy firm.

Elegant and very personable, Julienne is in her early forties and has progressed rapidly in her career. Though her technical skills are excellent, she needs to improve her leadership approach. She finds delegating very difficult and routinely takes on too much work. However, PDC has a lot of faith in Julienne and wants her to progress further. Her boss has encouraged her to have some coaching to focus on her development as a leader.

DOI: 10.4324/9781003613961-12

Now, she's sharing her story with me.

When she was only 17, Julienne explains, she went to the United States on a scholarship to study science. It seemed an amazing opportunity – a golden ticket for adventure and discovery, which also meant leaving her parental home at a time of crisis, when her parents were in the process of divorcing. However, after a couple of years, she had to leave the course quite unexpectedly and go back home: her scholarship wasn't renewed, and she didn't have the financial means to continue.

Julienne decided to change direction, mainly for pragmatic reasons. She found a course in economics that sounded interesting and managed to enrol in the university in her hometown. She went to live in a flat with her siblings, as the family home didn't exist anymore. She was able to earn a living very quickly and never looked back. After a few years in small financial companies, she joined PDC where she settled in well and felt very welcome.

I was struck by Julienne's ability to shake off her disappointment about the abrupt interruption of her American adventure and her capacity to get on with what was in front of her, apparently without resentment or bitterness. She seemed to live very much in the present, admitting, 'I work very fast and expect people to work at the same pace, but unfortunately they don't...'

She could digest figures and numbers very quickly, so it was tempting to take on a lot of work herself or to rescue situations and deal with delays caused by members of her team. There was a big gap between her and the people she managed, made even larger by her centralized approach. Julienne struggled to slow down and help her team develop at their own pace. Her premature step into adulthood had given her an extra edge and the capacity to get on with the task in hand, though it made it more difficult for her to include others. She was used to being self-reliant and struggled with the idea of depending on other people, as she'd had a limited experience of dependency on others while she was growing up.

The focus of the coaching was about learning to create more strategic space for herself as a leader and find ways of involving members of her team in her journey and tasks. This wasn't easy for someone used to driving in the fast lane. The role template she had internalized was coloured by her own background, and it was challenging for Julienne to appreciate people had very different work models and to understand how her staff experienced their roles. She had to learn to let them develop at their own pace, as well as involve them in all the key projects. Julienne's limited experience on how to be dependent on others made it difficult for her to allow and expect support and help from her team.

Through our conversations, she started to realize that a mature dependency, differently from primitive dependency, didn't mean surrendering or the abnegation of authority, and that mutually dependent relationships create the fabric of teamwork. She could be dependent on others without losing her personal authority. She gradually let other people take on more responsibility and became more accepting of their different pace and drive and their mistakes.

Julienne was finally able to put her energy into more strategic objectives, without feeling the constant urge to intervene, rescue and repair. Her psychological journey has made her more aware of what she brings to her role, as well as the impact of her early experience on the way she related to her team and inhabited her leadership role.

Mona, my next example, though quite different from Julienne, presented some similar patterns. Raised by impoverished emigrants, who had escaped their country of origin at a time of war, Mona had to learn how to fend for both herself as a young girl and for her parents – overcoming prejudice, overwhelming bureaucracy and a lack of basic essentials for many years. Though a success story, her experience of absence of parental support and influence – having had to parent her own parents – had shaped her view of her role and her leadership style.

PARENTING YOUR PARENTS

'I have a fundamental trust in this country's institutions', Mona tells me. 'I came with nothing, and thanks to the state's support, I had the opportunity to become who I am today. The state was my real parent. My parents weren't emotionally and practically able to parent me in this context'.

Beautiful, articulate and charismatic, Mona talks passionately about her story and background. Her gratitude about the opportunities she has had sounds very genuine. Now a medical consultant in a large hospital, her traumatic beginning seems very distant. She is profoundly loyal to the health service and her organization, though she struggles to lead her team, who don't always share her enthusiasm, commitment and capacity to get on with their demanding work.

Similarly to Julienne, Mona is very used to being self-sufficient and fast, and her team's slow responses and lack of grit surprise and deeply frustrate her. However, differently from Julienne, Mona expects people to be more responsive and engaged, and to be properly supported in running her department, regardless of its complexities and challenges. She sees herself very much as a leader and wants to delegate key tasks to members of her team. Yet, they seem quite reluctant to take up more responsibility and they tend to defer most of the complex and demanding tasks to Mona.

Her strong sense of self-belief is a mixed blessing: it has coloured her development and growth and protected her from setbacks and disappointments. Courageous and driven like a warrior, she struggles with the mediocrity and lack of motivation of some members of her team.

Vulnerability and leaning on others are quite unfamiliar to her, as from a young age she has had to parent her own parents, traumatized by the war, with little education and few skills. Her self-belief has acted as a shield against potential failures and obstacles, but it has also prevented her from being more emotionally available and empathic towards her staff or showing a degree of vulnerability.

Vulnerability means accepting and understanding one's limitations and shortcomings, yet it shouldn't prevent us from taking risks and accepting the consequences of this. The capacity to be vulnerable, without losing the sense of our own value and personal authority, is a great skill. It can create the emotional space for people to bring the whole of themselves to the workplace and to their role without fear of being judged or diminished. Sometimes, just acknowledging one's own mistakes, or owning up to anxiety in relation to a complex situation, can build the right climate for working together as a team and developing trust in each other and in the leader.

Mona, highly intelligent and perceptive, knows that, but finds it difficult to connect with other people's difficulties and vulnerabilities. Her sense of pride in what she has personally achieved, underlined by an element of omnipotence, prevails on her capacity to be more tune in with and sympathetic to others. Her loyalty to the health service and to her organization, strongly influenced by her experience of finding a home in the UK, also affects her approach to the team.

'Why can't they see how lucky they are?' she asks.

Our work together allows her to be more vulnerable with me, breaking the veneer of absolute self-belief and confidence. She starts to talk more openly about her doubts and anxieties, and how traumatic moments in her early experience still haunt her. Creating a space where she can explore her vulnerability helps her to engage more empathically with her team's struggles to be focussed, cooperative and fully involved in their current challenges. Their ethical compass is different from hers. Still, she can learn how to be more emotionally available to them, starting from where they are, rather than from where she believes they should be.

In the following three contrasting stories, the emotional absence is connected to the perception of being profoundly different from their original family: Pilar, *ejected* by her own family, who couldn't tolerate her difference; Khalid, *rejecting* his parents, ashamed of their humble background and Nadine, *running away* from a very authoritarian father and submissive mother.

EJECTED, REJECTING, AND RUNNING AWAY

Pilar, Khalid, and Nadine all shared a powerful sense of feeling profoundly different that made them eventually abandon their own tribe. However, their sense of loss, void, and lack of belonging greatly affected the way they took up their roles and developed their careers.

Pilar

'The gap between me and my family has become too big: here I am, based in London, in a senior and well-paid job, while the rest of my family is still in their small village, having made very little progress and feeling increasingly resentful towards me', Pilar explains.

This situation had started much earlier, when Pilar had shown great interest in her studies and a desire to develop a professional career. Though initially quite proud of her academic successes, both her parents and siblings became increasingly critical of her initiatives, aspirations, and successes. 'I never got it right', she says now, as if by embracing a professional career, she has betrayed her family and tribe through wanting to join a world they couldn't reach.

It was very painful for Pilar, who had been very close to her mother and older sister. She felt completely alone: she didn't belong to her tribe anymore, nor did she belong to the new world she had joined.

It was a painful journey: accepting the loss and considering ways of reconnecting with her family, as well as becoming more open to the professional world she had joined. She had lost her old identity without gaining a new one. She was frightened, as if there was no ground under her feet. She didn't know where to stand.

Our work together developed at a slow pace, since Pilar was extremely anxious and distressed; I had to be very careful not to steer her in any specific direction, just accompany her in her emotional journey. Eventually, she was able to make a few steps – reaching out to her mother again and showing more openness and interest in her colleagues at work.

She needed to recover the sense of agency she had lost – the result of the emotional absence of her parents and siblings, who had withdrawn their love and support. It took a long time for Pilar to feel secure enough in her own identity to socialize with colleagues and feel authorized to inhabit her role fully.

There is a paradox in the coexistence of the drive to be autonomous and separate and the need to belong and be attached: they are intertwined and we want both. It is difficult to forge one's own identity without maintaining an emotional link to our original tribe. It is our desire to belong that drives us to be part of a group that shares our values and history. Without it, we can feel lost and fear that there isn't another tribe to go to. Leaving our tribe or feeling rejected by it can become unbearable.

Pilar struggled to develop a separate identity for herself, mainly the result of the emotional split with her original family. Through the coaching sessions, she gradually started to recover some belief in herself and in her capacity for resilience. She was finally able to reconnect with her old tribe and take some steps closer towards the new tribe she had joined.

Unlike Pilar, Khalid had instead rejected his family for several years, too concerned with being 'infected' by their modest situation, provincial mindset, and expectations of him.

Khalid

'I feel guilty, but I can't be close to my family, I am ashamed about the way they are and the world they are in… I'm too different from them', Khalid admits.

Khalid's parents had been supportive of him going to university and helped him financially, despite their very limited resources. He embraced his new life away from the family as a great opportunity to carve his own destiny and distanced himself from his cultural and social roots. He became a successful lawyer who was very competitive and aimed high, though in a quite addictive way, incapable of saying no, always voracious and never content. Greed coloured his first professional years: what he achieved and did were never enough. He constantly wanted more.

At some unconscious level, Khalid acted out what the psychoanalyst Winnicott described as the 'need to kill the father', an inevitable stage for adolescents to gain maturity and independence (Winnicott, 1969). The rejection of his family and his background seemed like a delayed adolescent dynamic – an omnipotent stance to show his desire to stand 'solo', severing his emotional bond with the world he came from.

Khalid got in touch with me after a serious illness had forced him to take a long leave from work. He was shattered and confused, though quite aware that his approach to work, his drive, and competitiveness might be behind his long sickness.

He told me that he'd grown up in a small town, doted upon by his parents: the gifted and golden child, who had to be cherished and supported, but never challenged or made accountable. At university, he was initially quite idle and did very little work. He enjoyed the social life, mixing with people from much more well-educated and wealthier backgrounds. Then he had a lightbulb moment: he might fail his exams if he didn't start studying. This might sound like any ordinary student's story. It wasn't. Khalid became obsessed with studying and overcompensated for the time lost. He continued his studies and training with great determination, never wanting to miss an opportunity and never fully satisfied with his results.

Shame represents the emotional experience of inadequacy of the self, of feeling defective. Paul Hoggett makes an interesting distinction between *depressive shame,* a healthy emotion that can lead us to address our failures and shortcomings, and *paranoid shame,* which might generate a corrosive feeling of never being good enough.

Khalid's shame was related to a strong sense of being inadequate – never good enough – because of his family's modest background and lack of education. The only solution seemed to be to work as hard as he could to prove himself and to step away from his original world. However, it came at a great cost. Khalid's shame was coupled with greed – a compulsion to accumulate projects, training, and clients. He couldn't stop.

In our journey together, we brought to light the dynamics that had determined his obsessive behaviour, as well as the sense of guilt that was starting to emerge – probably a strong element behind his illness. The legal world, competitive and performance-driven, was another contributing factor.

Khalid gradually managed to shift from 'paranoid shame' to 'depressive shame', seeing his situation and background from a different perspective: his family's trust in him, though quite indulgent and idealistic, had been a key element in his development and professional success. Deep down, he wanted to prove to them that he was worthy of their trust and love. He came to realize that his shame had acted as a shield against the acknowledgement of his deeper feelings, including gratitude for his parents' support and affection.

Differently from Khalid, Nadine came from a very strict and unsupportive environment that she couldn't wait to leave behind.

Nadine

'I had to escape from a very authoritarian family regime', Nadine said. 'The chance came with university. I managed to support myself through it and never went back home'.

Nadine had a much more restricted life than her contemporaries, with very little joy. She felt imprisoned and unable to experience an ordinary childhood. When she finally went to university, she worked hard to be self-sufficient and kept her family at a distance.

I met her when she was in her forties, a successful executive in a large multinational. Coaching was offered to people at her level to prepare them for more senior roles.

I noticed how, underneath her confident approach, there was an emotional distance – she seemed guarded and reluctant to engage at a feelings level. Then, in one of our coaching sessions, a crisis emerged: she had made a mistake and had been criticized by her boss. As a result, her confident veneer started to crack. She felt devastated, as if her whole world had started to collapse and her diligence, commitment and focus had been wiped out by this incident. She was sure now that her colleagues perceived her as weak and incompetent.

It was at this point that she told me her story, mentioning the absence of warmth, encouragement and affection in her original family: 'I don't have a single photograph of me as a child. Taking photographs wasn't something my family did – too self-indulgent and superficial, I guess…'

Despite her emotionally deprived childhood, Nadine did well at university and built a good career for herself quite rapidly. Conscientious and focussed, she was well liked in her organization and seen as an asset to her team. However, the absence of a deep emotional bond with her parents had left a scar that reopened at times of crisis and under stressful situations. Then, she froze and felt insecure, losing her confidence and belief in her ability to cope.

Nadine is a poignant example of the impact of an early 'disturbed attachment' on adult life. Our childhood experience of attachment to parental figures influences our approach to the world, our sense of security and vulnerability and our resilience in relation to loss and life's challenges. It is the internalized 'attachment' that gives us the strength to face life's ups and downs. Nadine wasn't emotionally 'held' by her parents – she didn't experience what Winnicott described as a 'holding environment', a secure place provided by the mother for the emotional growth of her baby.

Nadine is still struggling with her internal vulnerability and lack of resilience, though, through the coaching, she has developed a better awareness of what can trigger her anxiety and is learning how to prevent getting overwhelmed by stressful situations. She knows she has to live with this internal insecurity and self-doubt, though she doesn't have to succumb to it.

Differently from Nadine, Tom's story is not about serious emotional neglect. It is about a more subtle form of neglect: his parents were never fully there for him.

THEY COULDN'T SEE ME…

Tom, the second of three children, was brought up in a very comfortable home environment. Despite the material comfort, he felt the emotional absence of his parents deeply: they weren't there for their children and particularly not for him, the middle child, being too preoccupied instead with their careers, their relationship with each other and the extended family.

'I was there, but they couldn't see me…' Tom said.

Tom, very personable and warm, wants to leave his job where he feels increasingly frustrated. His public relations (PR) agency has become too large and hectic, and he feels disconnected and overlooked. The PR agency has been his main job after graduation: he has been there too long.

Though I am impressed by his affability and friendly manners, I am also surprised by his lack of clarity and focus. He jumps from subject to subject and struggles to stay centred. He seems very confused and unclear about what he wants.

A few years ago, Tom decided to move far away from his family and live in a different city, as a sign of his independence and separateness. However, he still constantly talks about his siblings and parents as if he hasn't really left them behind. There is an adolescent flavour to his relationship with his family – seeing his life always through their lenses; a grown-up young man unable to leave the 'family home'. Tom is also constantly looking for mentors, therapists and coaches – adult figures that can parent him – trying to fill an absence that could never be filled.

I wondered how his parents' lack of psychological presence – the capacity to be fully there – without being too preoccupied with their own issues – has affected his own capacity to be fully there in his work and role. He never experienced his parents being entirely engaged with, or focussed on, him and his siblings, and he now struggles to find his centre, as if the lack of attention in his childhood has shaped the way he relates with the world of work. His lack of focus seems to repeat a familiar pattern: the difficulty of being emotionally present and fully engaged.

I didn't make much progress with Tom as he wasn't ready to commit to work with me. He was restless and already looking to move on to someone else. I was left wondering if he would finally find a parental figure who could fulfil his desire for focus and emotional presence, enabling him to stop his restless journey.

As shown in all the above examples, regardless of their differences in contexts and personalities, a lack of early parental attachment or poor psychological presence can deeply affect people's confidence, resilience, and personal authority in their work role. However, making the connection with their early experience, and identifying and recognizing unhelpful patterns can lead to significant positive changes.

The coaching journey, when fully embraced, can provide the transitional space in which to sketch out a course for the future – acknowledging the dynamics of the past and building a path for development and transformation.

Building a shared context and co-creating something new together are an essential part of the consultancy journey. This process can generate anxiety both in the client and in the consultant; it is an interactive process that requires openness, acceptance of vulnerability and a degree of humility. The challenge for both client and consultant is to engage with the uncertainty of the journey without trying to get to the destination too hastily – what the poet Keats has described as 'negative capability', a particular ability to be in the middle of uncertainties without pressing for answers and certainty.

In the next chapter, I explore the experience of not feeling part of an organizational or professional family, connecting it with the dynamics of adoption and fostering.

CHAPTER 10

We Are Not Family

Some teams or departments don't experience themselves as 'family' or aren't perceived as 'blood relatives' – there is a conscious or unconscious ambivalence about their existence and the legitimacy of their work and tasks. Their organization 'in the mind' (see Chapter 1) is often quite different from the organization they are part of, as if they don't share the same DNA.

'I could work here for another twenty years, but I'll never be seen by clinicians as a blood relative, just as step-sibling working alongside them. I'll never be fully part of their family', a senior administrator of a mental health clinic once told me.

Their situation reminds me of the dynamics of adoption and fostering, and the complexities of not being biologically related to one's family: the feeling that something fundamental is missing and can't be replaced even by loving and committed adoptive parents; the yearning for birth parents and the profound sense of loss that adopted and foster children so often experience.

The examples I will discuss in this chapter reflect these dynamics and show how these experiences have played out in the way these individuals take up their roles and on a team's sense of identity and belonging.

However, the first story I'm going to be sharing, though related to these dynamics, is slightly different. It is about a 'blue blood' organization that sees itself as being somewhat above ordinary organizations, a special and privileged entity whose feelings of 'superiority', not always conscious, have an impact on its lack of connection with the 'extended family' – such as organizations working in the same or related fields – and on its capacity to review its own practices, learn from others and embrace change.

DOI: 10.4324/9781003613961-13

A DYNASTY

There is a lively atmosphere around the table; it's a beautiful summer's day and people feel quite energized and optimistic. It's the first meeting in person of the executive team, after the long exile of the pandemic.

I share their excitement to be there, finally leaving behind the world of virtual meetings. The day goes well, though people seem quite reluctant to discuss their differences and their feelings about each other. In the individual consultancy meetings of previous months, they were able to express some criticism and doubts about their organization and each other in a much more frank and open way. They talked about how privileged they were, the great degree of autonomy they enjoyed and their difficulties in engaging with each other at a deeper level. 'Our meetings are very transactional, full of items with no space for reflection', Mandy told me. However, in this team context, it feels challenging for them to engage in difficult conversations.

The session ends, people comment positively about our work together and start chatting with each other. I leave the room for a few minutes; when I come back everyone has gone. Nobody is there to see me out. I feel puzzled to be discarded so quickly, as if they couldn't be bothered to say goodbye properly. Still, this feeling doesn't spoil the experience of having enjoyed a constructive day and the thrill of having finally met people in person.

At the end of the summer holiday, I get in touch with the team to arrange another session. After several promptings, I receive a short response:

> Your input has been very helpful in getting us started and we now feel more confident to continue our development on our own. At a time when we are still careful about finances, it would feel unwise to continue paying for external support.

I am stunned, quite hurt and angry. The consultancy should have continued for much longer. It all feels very transactional and emotionally detached. I have to insist on arranging a final session with the director. I don't want to be dismissed via email, and we need proper closure.

It is then that I reconnect with my experience at the end of the meeting in the summer. My feeling of having been prematurely disposed of was definitely spot on! Wishing to engage positively with this assignment, I didn't listen carefully to the 'music behind the words': I didn't want to 'hear' their resistance and ambivalence towards the consultancy process.

What went wrong?

Arrow is a highly respected and well-known organization, very much part of the establishment. Its focus is on social justice – it provides policies and consultation to organizations in the public and charity sectors. Though a wealthy organization with large reserves, it must now demonstrate financial prudence as well as develop the capacity to raise more funding.

The consultancy with me was initiated by Human Resources after an internal survey identified several challenging issues and dynamics within the organization. However, the pressure to live up to their reputation played a part in their difficulties around reviewing and reflecting on their team dynamics and practice and in their ambivalence about confronting what they needed to change and do differently.

They expect and are expected to demonstrate brilliance and forward-thinking and to provide leadership on social justice at a national level. Most of the senior staff are Oxbridge graduates and have a strong commitment to public service. Their 'privileged' status and external and internal expectations get in the way of them developing a more self-reliant and entrepreneurial approach. It's hard for them to accept dependency on and learning from others. Accepting dependency on others would have required a degree of humility that didn't seem to exist in their organizational imprint. Their mandate to 'influence' and lead on social justice got in the way of them developing a more self-critical and reflective approach.

The premature ending of my consultancy with them was evidence of their apprehension about taking up, even temporarily, a dependent position – being the client rather than the provider – and their struggle to trust someone else's professional experience. They seemed unable to accept that somebody different, outside their world, could make a useful contribution to their situation and challenges. It wasn't possible for them to develop a closer and in-depth engagement with the consultancy project and with me.

Arrow's position above ordinary 'family dynamics', their investment in maintaining a position of superiority – 'the dynasty' – even if at an unconscious level, was their Achilles' heel. The executive team's difficulty in exploring their team and organizational dynamics, and their inability to be more vulnerable with each other and with me, prevented them from embarking on the change they needed to face. Like an aristocratic family who had lost their lustre, they were struggling to move on and to find new ways of engaging with the current world and with each other.

In my desire to secure this assignment, I neglected early signs of their ambivalence: as a result, our work together was lukewarm from the start – they never fully engaged with me. Maybe there was an arrogance on my part, too: that I could win them over and make them see the consultancy was worth a real try. Though an initial ambivalence from the client could be a useful antidote to excessive expectations, idealization and potential collusion, my interest in the work had made me less tuned in to their lack of willingness to be emotionally engaged in the process.

On their part, the premature ending also showed the weak leadership of their director who, not just in this situation, was often indecisive and unclear about the direction of travel. Her distinguished research background wasn't enough to enable her to step successfully into a demanding leadership role among very competitive and rivalrous colleagues. Not surprisingly, the director left a few months after the abrupt ending of my assignment.

As in many other occasions, the consultancy provided a stage where organizational dynamics were acted out, though, in this case, I wasn't allowed to help my client to unpack and understand them.

Instead, they simply came on a date with me without any desire to commit in the long term…

ALWAYS AN OUTSIDER

While Arrow's difficulties in creating an inclusive sense of cohesion and accepting the input of others sprang from a sense of entitlement and from an expectation of excellence, several of my clients have struggled with the feeling of being outsiders, never fully recognized by their organization or never entirely able to authorize themselves in their roles – constantly perceiving themselves as temporary citizens, holding a visa, never a passport. The following two vignettes describe this dynamic.

The first concerns Amir, a successful medical consultant, who had spent his professional life in the UK. A gifted physician, he had reached an important position as head of an endocrinological department in a renowned hospital. However, despite his successful career, he had never felt fully 'at home', an internal voice constantly telling him he was missing out on opportunities that were available to his British colleagues but never to him, the 'outsider'.

Coming from a distinguished family of physicians wasn't a sufficient shield to protect him from perceived and real prejudices. Though he had created a tight-knit professional family within his department, he often felt misunderstood or overlooked in the larger system and struggled to make significant connections with peers and key players.

Lucy, on the other hand, had put her humble roots behind her to fully embrace her status as a successful scientist. Though her family had supported her all the way, she now felt awkward towards them, at times even embarrassed. She wanted to assert her difference and separateness from a world where she felt she didn't belong anymore.

Lucy was keen to become a full member of her adoptive family – the network of highly successful professionals she had now joined – and wished to distance herself from the 'social shame' of coming from an uneducated and modest background. However, a growing anxiety and sense of guilt had started to contaminate her sense of self and professional confidence. It was at this point that she decided to seek some help.

In both situations, the emotional split between their family of origins and their 'adoptive' family had affected Amir's and Lucy's sense of identity and belonging. The lack of grounding in their professional life had also reverberated in their personal life.

Amir's anger and frustration towards his adoptive family, though at times justified, had made it difficult for him to convey, outside his department, the depth of his experience and his seniority. His resentment and feelings of being left out had created a barrier with other colleagues and the leadership of the hospital, preventing him from fully engaging with his organization.

In contrast, Lucy's distance from her family of origin, and her desire to join a more shiny and prosperous adoptive family, had left her on unstable ground – as if she couldn't find a firm base or sense of identity. Moving away from her origins and background had generated an anxiety and guilt she couldn't manage, as she was still emotionally attached to her parents and fully aware of their support through the demanding journey of her becoming a scientist.

In my work with both Amir and Lucy, we tried to bridge this emotional split. Amir started to recognize his part in wanting to maintain an outsider position and his need to project all the rejection onto 'others', without acknowledging his own desire to reject the hospital's establishment. For Lucy, it was important to reconnect with her feelings of affection for her family and realize they shared more in common with her than she thought, despite the gap between them in education and wealth.

Though some of these dynamics continue, both Amir and Lucy have learnt to navigate them in a more thoughtful way and have achieved a better integration between their 'adoptive' and 'birth' families.

As in real adoptions, the most successful and resilient experiences are the result of the capacity to interweave the lives and stories of both adoptive and birth parents, creating a shared narrative and tapestry for all involved.

The feelings of being adopted in a professional environment shouldn't be seen as necessarily negative, if they were embraced as a reality and a difference that can be managed, recognized and at times used as an advantage. Working through feelings of rejection or lack of recognition is essential for coming to terms with a reality that can't be changed – like adoptions in real life – but can be experienced as a different perspective and position that can potentially add to and complement the core organization.

The example that follows next describes instead the challenging dynamics of a complex 'adoption'.

AN 'ACQUISITION' THAT WENT WRONG

It all started as an interesting experiment: the acquisition by a private mental health company of Novi, a niche provider of specialist services for adolescents.

Though Novi had a reputation for being quite controversial in their approach, the buyers thought it could provide a growth area for their business at a time of great financial instability.

The host organization was a well-established private clinic for patients with mental health problems, which had pioneered psychotherapy decades ago, long before it came into the mainstream.

The clinic's history of having faced many financial difficulties, as well as many challenges to their own approach, and ethos, was a strong motivation for acquiring this small service and giving it a 'home'. Though Novi's methodology didn't seem particularly complementary to their approach and practice – they were more traditional than them and more behavioural focussed – the leadership of the clinic trusted Ellie, Novi's founder, an experienced and well-respected psychologist, who was very optimistic about the future of this 'adoption'. Giving Novi a home also symbolized the clinic's desire to both be and be seen as open-minded and inclusive. And there was undoubtedly a need for more services for adolescents in the community they served.

The initial phase generated a lot of interest; Novi was viewed as an interesting addition to what the clinic had to offer. Patients had the opportunity to benefit from several diagnostic and counselling sessions before beginning their treatments. This 'adoption' started to yield some encouraging results.

After a few years, Ellie decided to retire. Jonathan, a younger consultant with substantial experience in the treatment of adolescents, became the leader of the service. He didn't have a background in psychotherapy and came from a different tradition, more behavioural and medically focussed.

Despite his credentials and experience, the clinic leadership was quite sceptical towards him and kept him at arm's length. Jonathan was also quite ambivalent about the clinic's ethos. A 'non-believer' in psychotherapy, he welcomed the opportunity to work independently.

As the demands for the service grew, his team likewise started to expand, creating a more demanding and complex system to manage. Their approach was also the focus of contrasting views among parents' organizations, other services and the health authority. Their methods were quite controversial and the pressure was mounting…

Suddenly, the service started to be inundated with demands without having the resources to deal with them. Alongside this, there was attention from the local press, pointing fingers at the organization and their 'adopted' service.

The situation was becoming untenable and the clinic's leadership decided to close the service and cut their losses. Their reputation was at stake, and the financial benefits of the growing service weren't worth the trouble it had brought.

So, what went wrong?

When I started to consult to Novi, the adolescent service felt like a start-up. It had all the characteristics of a new venture: a team that was enthusiastic, naïve and strongly convinced of their uniqueness. There was a widespread sense that they were doing something very special that would enhance the lives of troubled adolescents. Their excitement was mixed with a degree of arrogance, particularly towards people who questioned their methods and approach. They were reluctant to engage with different points of view. There was a strong flavour of adolescent dynamics in the way they related to the host organization and the community around them (see 'Team as a sponge', in the Glossary, page 125).

'Why did you join this team?' I asked a senior member of Novi.

'It's so interesting, it's never dull', I was told.

There was a loose sense of accountability and the interface with the clinic's leadership became increasingly fraught. Novi was never fully adopted by the clinic. Their existence and presence were initially seen as an interesting addition to what was on offer. Gradually, the interest in the service diminished; it was 'tolerated' as it was bringing in a substantial revenue that the clinic badly needed.

Towards the end, under the mounting criticism, inside and outside the organization, Novi became 'persona non grata' – an adoption that hadn't worked out. Jonathan's ambivalence towards the clinic's approach also had a strong impact on the lack of integration and Novi's alignment with the clinic's ethos and objectives. Novi never felt part of the clinic family, nor was it seen as an integral part of it.

Something essential was missing: the belief that, even if they weren't blood-related, they could still be part of the same family.

As an adopted child, unable to establish a trusting relationship with significant adults, Novi never managed to feel fully supported nor properly 'seen' and understood by the clinic. The clinic's leadership – 'the adoptive parents' – though initially curious and open to this new venture, gradually lost their interest in it and tried to distance themselves from this troubled adopted child who didn't behave in the way they wanted.

The lack of integration into the main organization was at the route of Novi's final 'expulsion'. It had become too challenging to work together and try to share a common purpose.

In the examples described the issue of identity was key: the adoptees' sense of not feeling really part of the professional families they have joined. Their difference of contexts and expectations was overlooked, and several complexities minimized – creating a perfect storm between ambition and aspirations and the inability, at both the individual and organizational levels, to recognize early on the challenges these 'adoptions' entailed.

They also carried the 'stain' of being different that – as for adopted and fostered children – can make you more vulnerable and less confident in your ability to engage with the turbulence of the work environment.

In the following chapter, I discuss the complex and often painful journey of leaving an organization and the emotional impact on the individuals involved.

CHAPTER 11

Falling Out of Love

Divorce is always a period of emotional turmoil, loss and grief. It can carry feelings of failure and broken promises – a sense of wasted years and bad emotional investments. It can also represent a mature decision and a necessary evolution or an act of courage and self-preservation.

Several of my clients have experienced similar feelings in their separation or 'divorce' from work, even when they were the ones who decided to leave: they have had to come to terms with their sense of betrayal for moving on and deviating from their original ideals, while also experiencing a great sense of relief and hope for a new chapter in their professional life.

The way they have approached leaving their job has been inevitably coloured by their own personal history with separations and loss and by the way their organizational environment has responded to their wish or decision to leave.

The stories in this chapter are all quite different, though all share the struggle of letting go of an environment that has been someone's professional home, despite having been often unhappy, unfulfilled or highly stressed there for a long time. As with failing marriages, it has been very challenging for them to admit 'defeat' and to accept the inevitability of a separation.

My role as a coach has been to accompany them on this journey – supporting, prompting and challenging them when they've found it difficult to face the reality of a toxic work environment or of a too demanding or impossible task. I have also helped them to face the 'symptoms' related to their stressful situation that they have underestimated or ignored for a long time.

My first example concerns Jim, who was brought up in a very strict religious environment that it took him years to leave behind. When he finally started to recognize that he needed to leave his organization too, feelings from the past started to re-emerge and he struggled to negotiate and plan his exit.

DOI: 10.4324/9781003613961-14

AN IMAGINARY PRISON

'I have always had a very strong sense of family. The strict religious group in which I grew up was intertwined with my own family. When I left the group, I was treated and felt like a traitor', Jim told me.

He looked young for his age and had a very warm and confident manner. It was easy to communicate with him and identify with his situation and dilemmas. I immediately felt a connection with him; I could see how it was easy for people to trust him.

Jim had been part of Rond, an organization caring for autistic children, for almost 15 years. He had developed his professional skills as an art therapist there and felt very appreciated and included from the start. He experienced a strong sense of loyalty and gratitude towards Rond, which had provided him with a stable professional home for a long time. However, the last couple of years had been extremely difficult and demanding; he had been given too many roles and too much responsibility, and he'd struggled to respond to such pressure and expectations.

> I have always been surrounded by people double-jobbing, so it was natural for me take on many roles without realizing the mounting stress it caused me. It was a shock when I became ill and had to take a long period of sick leave

he said now. He had ignored his symptoms – his constant tiredness and frequent headaches – for too long.

Rond was grappling with meagre funds and increasing demands from their clients and community. It had set the bar too high and now the organization felt overwhelmed and unable to respond to their clients' needs. Jim was aware of this challenge and had struggled for many months to juggle his clinical role with the increasing demands of his management and supervision roles. There was no joy in his work anymore, but he felt an internal pressure to carry on. His sense of duty and loyalty to the organization kept preventing him from taking a decision about leaving. He knew how difficult it would be to replace him and the time it would take.

When he approached me, he was already at a tipping point: it became clear to me that Jim needed to leave his organization. His job had become untenable; he had too many roles and the organizational task seemed unachievable.

He initially appeared open to the idea of leaving Rond. We discussed possible options and futures, and he seemed in a good position to move on and create new opportunities for himself.

However, there were always excuses to postpone his decision – a mortgage to pay, the arrival of new members of staff, or the fear of abandoning his boss at a time of crisis. Underneath all this there was the anxiety of being disloyal: of being seen as a traitor by an organization that had embraced him and fostered his development and growth.

At a deeper level, there was also the dread of repeating the emotional experience of leaving his religious strict setting – something that had marked his approach to groups and organizations. He had similarly been a member of this secular 'sect' for many years, and it felt unimaginable to him to be able to leave without creating a major rupture.

As a result of our work together, he was able to identify what was holding him back, recognize his position had become unsustainable and develop an interesting plan for his next chapter. It wasn't an easy journey – coloured by the guilt of abandoning his organization and worries about his future.

Jim has now finally handed in his resignation, after several changes of heart and much anxiety. The 'divorce' process has been painful, full of hiccups and interruptions. But, at last, he realized the gate was open – and it was up to him to walk free.

Whereas Jim was trapped by his concerns about what others would think, Alina's personality made it difficult for her to leave. Her stubbornness made her stay in her organization for too long, despite mounting evidence of an increasing organizational toxicity and the reluctance of the leadership to engage in any meaningful change. Her lack of confidence about possible futures for herself and weak self-esteem were also strong contributing factors to her difficulty in leaving.

EXPULSION

Alina frowned as she told me, 'I can't give in now and let them win after all my efforts to put students' mental health at the top of the agenda'. She spoke quickly, as if in a hurry to deal with her challenging situation – she was running out of time.

As the head of pastoral care in a large inner-city college, Alina had been feeling trapped and angry. She couldn't see a way out of her organization. She had made several attempts to address the widespread perception of pastoral care as being an insignificant appendix of the institution. She viewed it as a systemic problem: the college considered her department as a place to dump some of the most challenging and complex students, without any real wish to address and understand the issues and dilemmas they presented. Though a split between pastoral and academic roles is not unusual – and often an indication of anxiety around engaging with students in a more holistic way – in this college, the lack of integration and collaboration was particularly acute.

Alina's assessment was correct. The organization felt the pressure of producing successes: they couldn't confront failures. There were increasing pressures on the college leadership to produce positive outcomes and results.

When I first met Alina, I was impressed by her commitment and innovative ideas. She seemed very passionate about her work and determined to develop a better awareness of mental health within her institution and beyond. After a series of incidents involving some students and members of staff, our work took a different turn. What was originally a space for development became a 'crisis hub' – Alina brought a constant wave of difficult scenarios and challenging relationships to our sessions together. She was often tearful and visibly distressed.

The main theme was the lack of empathy and understanding of the students' emotional struggles from the academic departments. She felt her team was asked to fix their problems quickly and 'return' the students to them repaired and fully functioning. There was also the issue of limited time and space for the students to engage with their services at a pace they could manage.

Nothing seemed to shift and develop in the desired direction, and Alina's position within the college became increasingly untenable. She felt marginalized and powerless. She also seemed incapable of reaching a compromise; she kept the battle going, despite feeling progressively disheartened and very isolated. Her anger was palpable, but she couldn't stop protesting.

After several unsuccessful battles, she was ejected.

A sense of anger towards institutions in general coloured her experience and affected her capacity to fight back more constructively. Her ambivalent relationship with institutions was connected to her early life in Eastern Europe. There was a pervasive feeling that institutions couldn't be trusted, and she was always very suspicious of people in authority. Her internal 'historical' experience of mistrust was reactivated by the approach taken by the college's leadership, which she viewed as too rigid and lacking in empathy.

Alina never felt completely confident: an internal voice often reminded her of her shortcomings rather than her potentials and talents, an old scar from her childhood when she was often negatively compared to her more gifted siblings. This was something she had partly overcome through moving country and developing a successful career in the UK, though the critical internal voice never fully left her.

Her anger was her Achilles' heel – it prevented her from facing reality in a more pragmatic way and finding some middle ground. Her self-doubt added an extra edge: the fear of not being able to create a different future for herself. Therefore, leaving felt impossible. The battle had to go on.

For my part, I felt quite ineffective too, mirroring Alina's feelings about her role. I couldn't help her to let go and move on. My voice was heard but not listened to. I could only accompany her on this difficult journey.

However, we did continue to work together after she left the organization. She initially felt wiped out, defeated and sad about the whole experience. However, she managed to pick herself up, gradually detoxifying from that difficult period and situation, and started to engage in new projects, this time more cautiously and in a less immersive way. She had become more aware of her 'valency' for fighting and of the powerful influence of her childhood experiences on her current role and situation.

She also had to come to terms with the fact that she had been 'divorced' by her organization, rather than having been able to leave the organization herself. She had to carry the scar of having been ejected.

In contrast, Pippa, the protagonist of my next story, was able to make a positive decision to leave her organization, though after several intense and troubled months.

ANXIETY ABOUT FAILURE

'Thank you, Francesca, for all your support and guidance over the years, and most of all for helping me to leave...'

Pippa, the chief executive officer (CEO) of a large health trust, had been a high achiever; she had always expected to be in a very senior role and was interested in engaging with complex systems. Tall, articulate and assertive, she was used to commanding a room and gaining people's attention and trust. I remember feeling quite intimidated when I first met her, with her precise English, immaculate navy suit and confident manners, but I quickly warmed to her and learnt to see the person underneath the impeccable façade.

She had the drive, stamina and the self-confidence required for the top job. However, after the initial couple of years, her work was becoming increasingly difficult, though she couldn't contemplate leaving. She had always progressed in her career and never admitted defeat.

The context of the health service was full of challenges, and in particular her own trust: it was serving an extremely complex community with very limited recourses. Pippa's positive, no-nonsense approach had paid off at the beginning, but it was now viewed with some suspicion by an increasingly disillusioned workforce and a community that was angry and dissatisfied.

Maybe Pippa's leadership style had been too positive and head-on in an environment that had experienced too many setbacks, disappointments and broken promises. It seemed the organization needed a different kind of leader: someone with whom people could identify with, who was more tuned in to their specific environment and community, and, possibly, with a lighter touch.

Pippa became progressively aware of this shifting environment and the erosion of trust and transference towards her. She felt a profound disappointment about not having been able to produce more positive results and have a real impact – almost as if she had been incapable of carrying out her duty of care as a public servant. It was very painful for such an accomplished achiever – from school and university to several senior roles – to accept failure. It took a long time for Pippa to decide to leave and feel sufficiently hopeful that this decision would be good for both parties.

The idea that someone could be potentially more effective than her in this role was initially difficult for her to digest and quite distressing, particularly after all the time, thought and emotions she had invested in her job during the previous three years. Her idealized sense of herself struggled to accept this feeling of failure – rather like coming to terms with the idea that your life partner can find a more suitable companion and love elsewhere. Highly ethical in her approach, Pippa had put all her energy into this project, without realizing the effect it had had on her. She was emotionally and physically exhausted. Like Jim, my first example, she had ignored her symptoms for too long. It had been easier to turn a blind eye and carry on.

She had lost her husband the year before taking up her role with the Trust. This project then became her main focus and emotional investment. Echoes of the painful loss of her husband now resonated through the difficult process of separation from her organization: the fear and anxiety of losing something meaningful that couldn't be replaced.

However, Pippa's intelligence, self-awareness and capacity to review her circumstances helped her finally take a step back and look more objectively at her situation. Her health had also been affected by the long hours and daily challenges. She knew she had to quit.

After exploring several options, we started to design her next chapter.

Pippa took early retirement without any immediate plan to re-engage in any professional role. She decided to buy a cottage in a village she loved, joined a political party and didn't arrange to jump into any voluntary roles straightaway. She wanted to create a space to 'declutter', explore her desires for her future and enjoy the opportunities that the new 'divorce' had given her.

She really appreciated my help to see the 'divorce' from her organization as a chance to reinvent herself; she also had the capacity and maturity to understand that while she had partly failed in this project, she wasn't a failure.

A SILENT DIVORCE

The following is an example of 'silent divorce'. This term captures the complex dynamic where two people remain legally married, but one or both partners have checked out of the relationship.

The team I describe below had lost its purpose and sense of direction but had stayed 'in the marriage' partly for convenience and partly from fear of exploring and engaging in alternative scenarios.

Filter, a tech company, had lost two departmental bosses in the last three years. Despite their mixed feelings towards these individuals, the staff now felt abandoned and without a sense of direction. Their interest and engagement with their work had weakened and they felt somehow diminished and relegated to much less interesting jobs and roles.

The company had proudly positioned itself as a family-oriented enterprise, inclusive and caring towards its workforce, and a hub for creative thinking and innovation. However, the pressure of the market and a very competitive wider environment had gradually eroded their sense of family, cohesiveness and being special.

When we met in their posh newly refurbished office, the atmosphere felt very charged. After our initial informal chat, Marina, a team member, started crying. She was very unhappy; she felt under pressure and was often criticized. Then, one after the other, the rest of the team members started talking about an environment that was almost unrecognizable from the one they'd joined only a few years ago.

'We've moved from familial to corporate: our roles have become much more administrative, with little space for creativity and innovation', I was told. 'I fear we aren't out of the ordinary anymore, we have become like any other average tech company'.

Filter was always going to be a highly pressurized environment because of the very nature of its task: to produce innovative, cutting-edge technology. Now, though, the organization seemed to have lost its heart and purpose. The alignment with the original mission was gradually eroding – especially amongst this team.

'Why do you stay?' I asked.

People came up with different reasons: to give the organization a chance to change, loyalty to the overall project and lack of alternative options.

While they talked, I couldn't help feeling there was something missing: an absence of real emotional connection with the enterprise. The 'love' had gone: the relationship between this team and the organization seemed to have become quite transactional and sterile – like a marriage of convenience, where love was long gone.

I pointed out they still had choices, even if they were currently feeling trapped. 'There are always choices, if you allow yourself to see them…'

Their reluctance to consider alternative options was coloured by their anger at having been abandoned by their leadership and left to fend for themselves. It was as if leaving would mean giving in to the organization's lack of support and engagement with them; whereas staying was almost an act of resistance.

On the other hand, they all had very well-paid jobs that might be difficult to find in other companies. This added to their reluctance to consider other possibilities, though they struggled to discuss this openly.

My role now was to help them look at the dynamics of their 'silent divorce', and to explore the part they played in staying in an organization that had become increasingly distant from what they wanted and needed.

It can feel impossible to escape from the cage of a silent divorce. Routine, convenience and fear of facing an uncertain future act as invisible chains and prevent people from looking at choices and alternative scenarios.

The approach of 'together, but apart' could kill off the emotional investment we project into work. Work can have a strong containing function, provided we maintain a genuine alignment with the purpose of the organizations we are in. Purpose represents the essence of an organization, what it tries to achieve in the wider environment and what difference it aims to make. Losing our alignment with the organizational purpose can create an emotional vacuum and distance.

Marina and other members of her team are still processing the losses they will have to face if they eventually do decide to leave, as well as identify the gains and opportunities that other roles will give them, such as new challenges, fresh starts, but likely a lower salary…

The Italian word for choice is *scelta* and its Latin root is *scindere*, which means to cut. To choose, we must accept the inevitability of cutting ties to something that provides us with a sense of stability and continuity, even if love and commitment have long gone.

Despite moments of frustration and difficulty, work can help us to invest in something beyond our immediate surroundings and be a channel for our creativity and for developing our skill and talents.

In a world that feels increasingly uncertain, unpredictable and turbulent, divorce from work might seem like quite a threatening prospect and our past family histories might get in the way of reaching a positive separation that will allow us to build a different future for ourselves – dynamics I have described in the examples above. Therefore, 'together, but apart' might still feel a safer option.

Divorce from work, like divorce from a life partner, might be experienced as climbing a mountain – even if you are the person wanting the separation, as shown in my examples above. The anxiety of leaving a familiar situation, though coloured by unhappiness and frustration, can be very powerful, as is the fear of losing the sense of meaning attached to the situation we leave behind. It is essential to acknowledge the loss and allow space for mourning.

The coaching sessions have provided my clients with a transitional space where they have been able to bring their mixed and messy feelings and gradually find the courage to make a decision that has often proved not as painful as they thought.

They all had to separate their individual identity from their organizational identity, learning to develop new aspects of themselves to embrace their next stage.

My final chapter explores the role of older people in organizations and the dilemma of how to contribute and play a role in the workplace without occupying a position at the expense of younger generations.

CHAPTER 12

The Grandparent Effect

In the past, reaching old age was seen as a success. Today, ageing is mostly viewed as a failure.

As an older person still active in my profession, I have often asked myself what extra value I bring to my clients, students and younger colleagues. I have also wondered what I might lack, due to my advancing years.

At a time when appearing young and fit is an endless aspiration and objective, the value older people can bring to work, family and society is often overlooked. Old age can cause anxiety both in the young and in the old: the shadow of death and senility colours our attitudes towards ageing. There is a fear of people losing their focus, moving at too slow a pace, and struggling to engage with technology as 'digital immigrants'. Denial and fear of death can impair people's capacity to appreciate and engage with the benefit and power that full maturity can bring.

However, the wisdom and broader perspective acquired through experience can provide a 'psychological containment' in work and societal settings. What I have come to call the 'grandparent effect' can help to moderate extremes, provide a sense of history, and offer a context for innovation and development. As some psychologists have pointed out, in old age we can become 'our essential selves', embodying the Buddhist concept of impermanence associated with increased gratitude, equanimity, and savouring life.

ANXIETY ABOUT DEATH

In 1915, Freud wrote, 'We display an unmistakable tendency to "shelve" death, to eliminate it from life'. Has anything changed over a century later?

Jeff Bezos, the founder of Amazon, is one of the billionaires financing new start-ups aiming to understand why we age and how we might prevent it. The super-rich have invested vast amounts of money in rejuvenation technologies.

DOI: 10.4324/9781003613961-15

In her recent book *The Immortalists*, Kotowski gives an insightful account of 'Those who believe the end of age is within our grasp: the tech bros and billionaires who consider that our bodies are as programmable as the products they sell'. She talks about how the idea we might have a natural life span is perceived as defeatism or 'deathfism' (*FT*, 25 October 2025).

Is this a response of the super-rich to our anxiety about death?

The psychoanalyst Nina Coltart found herself increasingly interested in treating elderly patients, having discovered a particular quality in this work. She talks about their clear sense of need, intensity of devotion to work, their skill in recognizing shorthand opportunities and a reduction of embarrassment and shame.

Undoubtedly, anxiety about death increases in older age, as death gets closer to us both in phantasy and in reality. Getting older 'well' requires the capacity to mourn the loss of the mental and physical capacities of our younger selves. Accepting change always requires dealing with the loss of what is not there anymore and a capacity to engage with the uncertainty the new situation brings.

A FINE WINE IMPROVES WITH AGE...

Over the last ten years, especially recently, I have seen a shift in myself and in how my clients and students have responded to my interventions. They seem to show a deeper trust and a more tangible appreciation of what I offer. I can recognize their experience in my own response to older mentors and to my own father – the feeling of being understood and seen; the sense that nothing I might have shared or said could shock or shift their interest in me.

The Japanese have an expression for their active and healthy elderly: the 'young-old'. Anthropologists have suggested that grandparents have played an important role in human survival. The 'grandmother hypothesis' suggests that help from the maternal grandmother would lead to increased resources for the child, a higher survival rate and, ultimately, longer life expectancy for humans in general (Hawkes, 2000). Rather than being a burden to society, the post-productive generation could enhance the fitness of the group.

As older people, we can bring the additional value of our life experience: the invisible accumulation of life events that allows us to make more informed responses to challenging situations and helps to give us a broader perspective. Older people are often sources of knowledge and mentors, can mediate between grandchildren and the middle generation, and contribute to the child's well-being in a significant way.

If we translate these attributes into the workplace, the older generation can provide similar benefits to organizations, which I refer to as 'the grandparent effect'. Their key quality is their capacity for 'containment' based on their experience of the complexity of organizational life through many years of experience in different emotional and organizational contexts.

The concept of 'containment' relates to the capacity of the mother to respond, tolerate, and transform her baby's distress. To be able to work effectively, we need to be part of containing structures that provide us with enough sense of 'holding' (see Chapter 3).

Sometimes, just the presence of an older person in a team can help others to feel more connected to the task and anchored to the workplace. Containment represented by the older person comes from their historical perspective: the feeling that crises and conflicts can be survived and dealt with.

The following vignette is an example of what I mean.

I recently consulted to a catering organization that was in great turmoil. The staff, all very young, in their twenties and thirties, had been particularly affected by the lockdown and had developed a strong resentment towards Nick, the founder of the company who was accused of not being sufficiently inclusive and innovative in his approach.

Their criticism of Nick, also in his thirties, made him distraught; as the organization's founder, he was very proud of what they have been able to achieve in a very competitive environment and with limited funds. He struggled to understand the staff's anger and took all their criticisms very personally.

A central focus of my consultancy with Nick became to help him to 'de-personalize' the negative feedback – trying to understand and unpack what made his staff feel so disgruntled and unhappy, rather than becoming increasingly defensive in his response to them.

I was certain the lockdown had been a key element in creating these negative dynamics: as young professionals at the beginning of their careers, the members of staff had found it particularly hard to stay away from work. Their motivation, passion, and dedication for the work didn't have an outlet anymore. Their frustration and anger were channelled towards the founder, who couldn't bear their resentment and felt increasingly hurt.

When lockdown ended and the organization resumed some normality, the tension, as I expected, eased – helped by Nick's growing ability to engage and tolerate their frustrations and demands. I became for Nick a trusted 'companion', who could support him as well as challenge him in his journey to move the organization forward.

This was one of my first consultancy projects in person after the pandemic. Despite some initial apprehension to re-engage with the 'real world', I enjoyed going there and immersing myself in this buzzy, creative, and young environment.

I often wondered if my age had a significant impact on the organizational dynamics, and on Nick in particular. Our difference in age was considerable, and I was very aware of the generational gap between us. I didn't feel distant or detached; I felt a deep connection with the organization and a strong empathy with Nick. However, I perceived something different from other consultancies, particularly when comparing this experience with my work with older leaders.

On reflection, I realized I took a 'grandparent' position in relation to the organization, providing the containment and wider perspective that Nick, the 'young, anxious parent', struggled to give to his team. As a 'grandparent', I implicitly communicated that I wasn't particularly affected by their disruptive dynamics, as I had engaged with similar challenging situations many times before. I was able to empathize with their difficulties without being put off by them or being afraid of them.

THE THIRD ACT: AGEISM IN THE MIND OR THE ILLUSION OF LIVING FOR EVER?

For older people, the anxiety of letting go and the fear of becoming marginal have always been at the centre of approaching retirement – though there is a more complex dynamic at play today, the consequence of longevity, longer life expectancy and advances in technology. This experience is increased by a context that, on the one hand, appears to offer endless opportunities, and on the other hand, is unpredictable and takes place within a society that seems anxious and fearful about engaging with fragility and old age.

The conscious or unconscious denial of one's own limitations and a primitive fear of annihilation also play a part in this dynamic. Staying on in a job and being 'greedy' by clinging on to employment helps to postpone facing what is perceived as being an uncaring and uncertain environment towards older people without a role or status, as shown in an incident that happened to a friend when he went to see a surgeon to discuss an imminent operation.

My friend looked frail and spoke quietly with a foreign accent. The surgeon was kind, though quite condescending in his manner. My friend mentioned he was still working and wanted to continue as long as possible. 'What do you do?' the surgeon asked, to which he replied, 'I'm a professor of economics'. The whole tone of the conversation changed: suddenly he was treated as an adult, and the infantilizing tone disappeared.

It is the fear of becoming invisible or irrelevant that can make older people greedy, sometimes occupying positions for too long and even robbing the younger generations of opportunities to grow into senior roles. It is also the lack of predictability that intensifies the anxiety of letting go.

Increasing longevity has provided a different landscape, creating new expectations and potentially fresh opportunities for the older generation in the workplace. This is reflected on the global stage, where some of the main players are now well into their seventies and eighties. In an article in the *Financial Times*, Lucy Kellaway talks about the widespread of ageism: 'Not only is age the poor relation in diversity policies, it is still acceptable in polite society to be rampantly ageist'. She observes how puzzling it is that the prejudice is not against people who are different to us: 'it is against our future selves' (*FT,* 16 January 2022).

'Ageism in the mind' can prevent people from benefitting from the experience, wisdom and broader perspective the older generation can bring. In addition to this, the illusion of endless opportunities can get in the way of developing relevant 'grandparent' roles in organizations and wider society.

My own experience of working with younger colleagues has been a major highlight of recent years. I have benefitted greatly from being exposed to the freshness of their perspectives, as well as to new ideas and interesting approaches. Their faster pace and digital competence, though at times intimidating, have forced me to be more alert and focussed. My predominant feeling has been of a very generative intergenerational collaboration.

> You have been there before – you are less anxious,' says a colleague of my generation, before continuing, 'However, in our field, energy comes from the freshness of our encounter with a client – ignorance is a strength. This might get diluted when we get older. Also, the competition and rivalry we experience with colleagues can be very energizing and creative. Getting older, we emotionally step back from it and lose some of the sharpness that competition brings.

The question is how we detect when we are losing our impact, and our contribution is becoming less effective. Can we acknowledge our difficulty in letting go of roles that have given us influence and pleasure – and recognize the tension between the wish to remain engaged and relevant, and the legitimacy of occupying a space that maybe shouldn't be ours anymore?

Conclusion

What could we learn from the stories in this book?

All my clients realized they needed a 'benign third', somebody external enough to their world to provide them with a reflective space. They understood they had to be challenged if they wanted to gain a deeper understanding of what lay behind their issues and dilemmas and learn to manage their desire for a quick solution to their difficulties. They were prepared to do the emotional work required to understand the roots and the undercurrents of what made them unhappy or dissatisfied in their work and role. This took courage, determination, and a genuine desire for change. For many it wasn't an easy journey, while others felt reinvigorated and ready to embrace the process. A few people struggled to engage and gave up before they were able to shift some of the dynamics at play and take positive steps.

As with the *kintsugi* technique, in most situations it has been possible to let the complex dynamics to surface, rather than conceal them, making them part of the whole story. Something to acknowledge, examine and try to understand rather than dismiss or cover up.

We have learnt how primary dynamics from our early experience have become part of our DNA, and how our internal representations of our own families and roles within them will always follow us like omnipresent shadows. Yet the process of identifying and understanding them can be transformational and can, in turn, help us to manage and come to terms with challenging family dynamics. In some cases, this understanding has provided closure and a sense of peace.

People have realized from their own experiences how family roles and positions, taken or given, inevitably become internalized templates for roles they assume or project onto others in the work context, shaping the way we relate to colleagues, bosses, and people we lead. We cannot erase these templates, though we can learn to manage them in more constructive ways.

DOI: 10.4324/9781003613961-16

Well-adjusted and loving family environments are also not immune from difficult dynamics and painful feelings. Being part of a family, our first organization, is complex. It's where we learn to relate to others, to deal with authority, rules, and boundaries. Families carry out a developmental task on behalf of society, and their capacity to contain helps to define the boundaries between the family and the external world. When there is a lack of containment because of a lack of emotional availability or abusive relationships, absence, or illness, childhood development can be derailed. Families, in their many diverse forms and shapes, create the emotional imprint we carry out all our lives. An imprint we can learn to understand and manage, but that we can't change.

A healthy attachment to parental figures in the early years is one of the most important ingredients for emotional stability in later life. Something some of my clients couldn't experience, because of their difficult beginnings. However, they had the determination and willingness to pursue interesting and demanding careers and had the courage and humility to look for help when they needed it.

My clients wanted to find their voice or develop a louder voice and to feel empowered to engage with their work situations differently. They wanted to regain emotional control over their work life, becoming the driver rather than a passenger. For some, the challenging experience of the global pandemic was a turning point that created the conditions or the crises that prompted a genuine desire for change – and the willingness to make this happen.

As I am writing these concluding sentences, I am expecting the arrival of my third grandchild. This book is dedicated to him and his older cousins. My own personal experience as a 'grandmother', both at a personal and at a professional level, has made me reflect, throughout the writing of this book, on the power of the family inside us: the joy, huge responsibility and sorrow families can bring. And how the issue of succession can be a source of grievance and disruption or the basis for a sustainable future if the old and the new generations are prepared to accept the losses and adjustments that inevitably come with change and the transference of power and responsibilities.

This book is also dedicated to all my clients who, through our work together and their openness and trust in me, have given me many opportunities for growth and development both in my personal and professional life. Thank you.

Glossary

Anxiety

Anxiety is a symptom of our fear of losing control of our rational self and of the risk of more irrational and primitive emotions taking over. They can be suppressed or split under the threat of becoming overwhelming.

There are also organizational anxieties related to the challenges of the organization's primary task.

Both individuals and organizations develop *defences against anxiety*. Some defences are necessary to deal with the complexities of our lives, some are dysfunctional.

- Menzies Lyth, I. (1988) *Containing Anxieties in Institutions: Selected Essays.* London: Free Association Books.

Attachment

Attachment originates in the bond between parent and child. The attachment figure provides a secure basis from which the child can explore the surrounding environment. The capacity for attachment defines the ability of individuals to develop relationships and trust in others. It is a 'primary motivational system' that operates through our lives.

- Bowlby, J. (1973) *Attachment theory, Separation Anxiety and Mourning.* London: Tavistock Clinic.
- Marris, P. (1993) *Loss and Change.* London: Routledge.

Authority

This refers to the right to make the ultimate decision, and, in organizations, to make decisions which are binding on others.

Obholzer points out that authority comes from three different sources: from above, within and below. Individuals and leaders can't exercise their full authority if they are not sanctioned from above and they are not legitimized by the people they manage and lead.

Authority from within is our capacity to legitimize ourselves in our role. It is connected to the nature of our relationship with the authority figures we have internalized – they can influence the way we take up our own authority and our relationship with authority figures in our work context.

- Obholzer, A. (2019) 'Authority, Power and Leadership', in Obholzer A. and Roberts V.Z. (eds) *The Unconscious at Work*. London: Routledge.

Boundaries

These separate the outside from the inside across which exchanges with the external environment take place. They need to be sufficiently solid to prevent confusion and disintegration and sufficiently permeable to allow the exchange to take place. Organizations are much less boundaried than they once were and the boundaries that do exist are more permeable.

- Cooper, A. and Dartington, T. (2004) 'The Vanishing Organization: Organizational Containment in a Networked World', in Huffington C. and Armstrong D. (eds) *Working Below the Surface*. London: Karnac.

Containment

The notion of containment relates to the capacity of the mother to respond to her baby's distress and to transform and tolerate her/his painful feelings – creating a 'holding environment' for the baby's development and growth.

To be able to work effectively, people need to be part of containing structures that provide enough sense of holding and context to develop their capacity to be creative and productive. The lack of organizational containment can have a disruptive effect on the individual or the group.

- Bion, W.R. (1984) *Elements of Psychoanalysis*. London: Karnac.
- Winnicott, D.W. (1971) *Playing and Reality*. London: Tavistock Publications (Reprinted Harmondsworth: Penguin Books, 1980)

Dependency

We can make a distinction between primitive and mature dependency. Primitive dependency is a frightening state of mind, looking for a reliable object to save us from danger, while mature dependency is an interactive process where differences are recognized and valued.

- Dartington, T. (2010) *Managing Vulnerability – The Underlying Dynamics of Systems of Care*. London: Karnac.

Emotions as data

In infancy, the baby communicates his feelings through cry or sounds. Parents, if emotionally available, can feel something of what the baby feels and can use it to respond appropriately.

In our adult life we can also experience other people's emotions. Staying with the emotions long enough helps us to discern their meaning. The capacity to understand and relate to these unconscious communications gives us important data to understand the dynamics at play, being alert and paying attention to feelings — our own and others' – rather than taking things at face value and reacting to them.

Using feelings as data can add valuable information that might not be available to us in other ways through what Armstrong called 'emotional intelligence' – a form of detective work.

- Armstrong, D. (2004) 'Emotions in Organizations: Disturbance or Intelligence?' in Armstrong D. and Huffington C. (eds) *Working below the Surface*. London: Karnac.
- Trainor, K. (2019) 'Feelings as Data', in *The Unconscious at Work*. London: Routledge.

Family patterns at work

We can find ourselves sometimes caught out by surprisingly strong and quite irrational emotions or by puzzling patterns of behaviour. The origins of such feelings and patterns often lie 'in the shadow' cast by early life experiences, beneath the surface of what we are aware of.

Our adult experience is rooted in those of our early years, which motivate our choices and drive our desire for certain professions and areas of work. Reflecting and developing self-awareness on how experiences from early life may influence present feelings and behaviours can have a significant influence on how we inhabit our work role and manage our experiences at work.

- Cardona, F. and Damon, S. (2019) 'Family Patterns at Work', in Obholzer A. and Roberts V. Z. (eds) *The Unconscious at Work*, London: Routledge.
- Klein, M. (1959) 'Our Adult world and its Roots in Infancy in Envy and Gratitude' in *The Writings of Melanie Klein,* volume 3 (1975), London: Hogarth Press.

How are you right?

Listening to how the other is right entails acknowledging other people's perspectives, even if they are substantially different from ours – asking the question 'What aspect of what they are saying fits with my experience?' This can create the opportunity for deeper understanding and for discovering new meanings.

- Shapiro, Eduard R. (2020) *Finding a Place to Stand.* Bichester: Oxfordshire, Phoenix.

Identity

From Latin *idem,* meaning the same – the capacity of feeling the same, having an internal coherence and continuity over time. It also involves the capacity for experiencing others as separate human beings.

Miller talks of the 'paradoxes inherent in our psychosocial being…the coexistence of the drive to be separate and autonomous and the need to be attached, to belong'.

- Miller, E.J. (1999) 'Dependency, Alienation or Partnership? The Changing Relatedness of the Individual to the Enterprise', in French and Vince (eds) *Group Relations Management and Organization.* Oxford: Oxford University Press.

Inner world and internal objects

The concept of an unconscious internal psychic space populated by mental representations connected with our early experiences with significant people and the external world.

- Klein, M. (1959) 'Our Adult world and its Roots in Infancy in Envy and Gratitude', in Colman A.D. and Geller M.H. (eds) *Group Relations Reader 2*. Wahington, DC: A.K. Rice Institute Series, 1985.

Kintsugi

This is a centuries-old Japanese repair technique which uses a Japanese lacquer dusted with powdered gold to restore broken ceramic and porcelain vessels. Rather than masking fractures, *kintsugi* highlights them with gold to tell an object's story. Items which have been restored using this technique are often considered even more precious than they were before.

As a philosophy, *kintsugi* is similar to the Japanese philosophy of *wabi-sabi*, which embraces the flowed or imperfect.

- Kintsugi, Japanese Repair technique, Japan house, London https://www.japanhouselondon.uk/read-and-watch/kintsugi/
- Kintsugi, Wikipedia

Lateral/distributed leadership

A more collaborative form of leadership that requires a different mindset and a particular understanding of the emotional challenges facing leaders in these settings, removing the protection of more hierarchical structures.

Lateral leadership can be psychologically demanding, as it is essential to be able to exercise personal authority without recourse to formal power, position or bureaucracy.

- Huffington, C., James, K. and Armstrong, D. (2004) 'What is the Emotional Cost of Distributed Leadership?' in Armstrong D. and Huffington C. (eds) *Working Below the Surface*. London: Karnac.

Mourning and change

Mourning is a psychological necessity. The management of change and transition depend on our ability to articulate the process of grieving.

Marris points out that grief is the expression of a profound conflict between contradictory impulses: to consolidate what is valuable from the past and at the same time to re-establish a meaningful pattern of relationships, in which loss is accepted. People's ability to articulate the process of grieving can give meaning to the present and make space for change.

- Marris, P. (1993) *Loss and Change* London: Routledge.

Oedipal dynamic

The Oedipus dynamics refers to the child's recognition of the parents' relationship with each other. It creates a *triangular space*, where the child is both a participant in a relationship as well as an observer of a relation between two people. This creates the basis for seeing oneself in interaction with others and considering other points of view while retaining our own.

The notion of *triangular space* can be applied to coaching and consultancy settings where different perspectives can be explored and considered.

- Britton, R. (1989) 'The Missing Link: Parental Sexuality in the Oedipus Complex', in *The Oedipus Complex Today: Clincal implications*. London: Karnac.
- Cardona, F. (2020) *Work Matters: Consulting to Leaders and Organizations in the Tavistock Tradition*. London: Routledge.

Holding environment

A concept developed by Winnicott.

The mother provides a holding environment: a secure place for her baby's development and emotional growth. As a result, the child is able to venture out and explore its environment.

This concept can be applied to groups and organizations, where we can feel held or not sufficiently held by our working environment.

- Winnicott, D. (1971) *Playing and Reality*. London: Tavistock Publi cations.

Holding the Centre

Gould talks of holding the centre as a core function of leadership and the emotional challenge of holding the centre in the mind.

The capacity to hold the centre is connected to the idea of resilience, holding on to the essence of the organization and maintaining a sense of wholeness.

- Gould, L. (2010) 'Barack Obama's post partisan dream: leadership and limits of the depressive position' in Brunning H. and Perini M. (eds) *Psychoanalytic Perspective on a Turbulent World*. London: Karnac.

Narcissism

Being in love with oneself. Taking a narcissistic position implies a denial of a need for dependence and a sense of omnipotence and self-sufficiency.

- Steiner, J. (2006) 'Seeing and Being Seen: Narcissistic Pride and Narcissistic Humiliation', *International Journal of Psychoanalysis*, 87, 939–951.

Old age

- Kotoski, A. (2025) *The Immortalists: the Death of Death and the Race for Eternal Life*. London: Penguin.
- Anthropologist Kristen Hawkes developed the concept of the 'Grandmother Hypothesis': post-menopausal grandmothers provide crucial food and childcare, allowing their daughters to have more children and increasing overall family fitness, thus ensuring their genes thrive.
- Hawkes, K., O'Connell, J.F., Blurton Jones, N.G, Alvarez, H. and Charnov, E.L. (2000) 'The Grandmother Hypothesis and Human Evolution', in *Adaptation and Human Behavior*. London: Routledge.

Open systems

This is a framework that looks at organization as *open systems*- the notion that any system can survive only by being open to the external environment. The boundary around the system needs to be both sufficiently clear and robust to separate the inside from the outside, and suitably flexible to allow the interchange with the external context.

If the boundaries are too rigid the system will eventually die.

- Roberts, V.Z. (2019) 'The Organization of Work: Contributions from Open Systems Theory', in Obholzer A. and Roberts V.Z. (eds) *The Unconscious at Work'*. London: Routledge.

Organization in the mind and family in the mind

This refers to the idea that each member of an organization holds a distinctive representation of the organization in their mind: a conscious or pre-conscious construct focussed on the emotional experience of task roles and purpose. It has also been described as 'the workplace within'.

Family in the mind refers to the internal representations of the family, part of one's inner world – held by different members of the family.

- Armstrong, D. (2018) *Organization in the Mind*. London: Karnac.
- Hirschhorn, L. (1988) *The Workplace Within: Psychodynamic of Organizational Life*. Cambridge: MIT Press.

Performativity

There is a growing culture of performativity with the emphasis on performance and on results. The anxiety raised by a culture of performativity leads us into a survival mode that prevents us from engaging with the meaning of what we do: 'We become ontologically insecure: unsure whether we are doing enough, doing the right thing, doing as much as others or as well as others, constantly looking to improve…' (Ball 2003)

- Ball, S. (2003) 'The Teacher's soul and the Terrors of performativity', *Journal of Education Policy*, 18(2): 215–228.
- Hoggett, P. (2016) 'Shame and Performativity: Thoughts on the Psychology of Neo-liberalism'. Tavistock Lecture

Perverse state of mind

The perverse state of mind, as described by Long, 'is not simply a deviation from normative reality. It has to do with individual pleasure at the expense of a more general good. It reflects a state of primary narcissism ... Perversion begets perversion ... because of the complicity of the accomplices and their subsequent denial and self-deception' (pp. 191–192).

- Long, S. (2002) 'Organizational destructivity and the perverse state of mind', *Organizational and Social Dynamics*, 2(2): 179–207.

Negative capability

It is a particular ability to 'be' in the middle of uncertainty, without pressing for certainties, facts and answers – a capacity to tolerate not-knowing without leaping into action.

- Keats, J. (1887) *The Letters of John Keats*. Oxford: Oxford University Press, 1952.
- Sievers, B. (Ed) (2009) *Psychoanalytic Studies of Organizations*. London: Karnac.

Psychological presence

This is the concept of being emotionally engaged with our tasks and roles. Khan links the personal engagement with the authenticity of working with one's real emotions. He identifies three main essential conditions to be psychologically present:

1. Not being too preoccupied with one's own issue.
2. Being involved in a meaningful task.
3. Feeling safe enough to employ 'the self without the fear of negative consequences'.

- Khan, W.A. (1992) 'To Be Fully There: Psychological Presence at Work', *Human Relations*, 45: 321–350.

Shame

Hoggett makes a distinction between *depressive shame*, a healthy emotion because it might lead us to address our failures and try to meet our goals, and *paranoid shame*, a more corrosive feeling of humiliation where failure means uselessness, feeling not good enough

- Hoggett, P. (2017) 'Shame in Organizations'. OPUS Lecture

Siblings

The concept of siblings has been neglected in psychoanalytic literature until quite recently. The influence and impact siblings have on our development and internal world is now more widely recognized.

- Coles, P. (2006) *The Importance of Sibling Relationships in Psychoanalysis*. London: Karnac.

Succession

Billington, M. (2013) 'The National Theatre at 50: Michael Billington's view from the stalls', *Guardian*

Cardona, F. (2021) 'Tribal Dynamics in succession', in *Psychodynamic Practice*

System-psychodynamic approach

This term refers to the marriage between psychodynamic ideas such as unconscious feelings, transference and countertransference, and systemic concepts such as boundaries, roles and tasks.

It is important for the practitioner to engage with both, trying to understand the dynamics under the surface, as well as paying attention to the organization as a system in the context of the wider environment.

Fundamental to a system-psychodynamic approach is the ability to be open to the experience and projections of the people we are consulting.

- Cardona, F. (2020) *Work Matters Consulting to Leaders and Organizations in the Tavistock Tradition*. Routledge: London.

The team as a sponge

The term 'sponge' describes the powerful way in which a team absorbs the central dynamics which operate within its client group, often without realizing it's happening. Understanding the 'sponge effect' can be translated in meaningful actions and changes within the team and help staff to reach a more mature approach to its task.

- Cardona, F. (2020) 'The Team as a Sponge: How the Nature of the Task Affects the Behaviour and Mental Health of a Team' in Cardona, F. (ed), *Work Matters: Consulting to Leaders and Organizations in the Tavistock Tradition*. London: Routledge

Transitional space

This is the space available to engage in transitional learning, away from the pressures of getting on with our job, perform and achieve our objectives. Coaching and consultancy are transitional spaces where to explore organizational and role dilemmas.

It is linked to Winnicott's original concept of 'transitional object' in relation to infant development.

- Amado, G. and Ambrose, A. (2001) *The Transitional Approach to Change*. London: Karnac.

Transference and countertransference

Transference is when we bring into a relationship something that belongs somewhere else.

Countertransference is our response to what has been projected onto us. In a consultancy setting, it could provide information about the emotional state of the client or of the client's organization

Trauma

The word trauma comes from the Greek, meaning piercing of the skin. It is the breakdown of an established way of going about one's life and of established beliefs about the predictability of the world.

Psychological trauma put us in touch with primitive anxieties such the fear of death. It can be experienced as an attack on attachment, provoking a sense of persecution and mistrust – a perception that our internal sense of good and safety is under threat.

- Garland, C. (2002) *Understanding Trauma: A Psychoanalytic Approach.* London: Karnac

Unthought known

Bollas describes as unthought known the emotional sense that a past dynamic influences our behaviour without consciously acknowledging it or knowing what it is. This unconscious dynamic might emerge at a later stage.

- Bollas, C. (1987) *The Shadow of the Object: Psychoanalysis of the Unthought Known.* New York: Columbia University Press.

Valency

The term valency – the affinity of some atoms to combine with others to form molecules – describes our propensity to be drawn into particular unconscious roles or behaviours.

- Bion, W.R. (1961) *'Experiences in Groups' and Other Papers.* London: Tavistock Publications.

References

Billington, M. (2013) 'The National Theatre at 50: Michael Billington's View from the Stalls', *The Guardian.*

Bollas, C. (1987) *The Shadow of the Object; Psychoanalysis of the Unthoughts Known.* New York: Columbia University Press.

Cardona, F. (2020) *Work Matters Consulting to Leaders and Organisations in the Tavistock Tradition.* London: Routledge.

Cardona, F. (2021) 'Tribal Dynamics in Succession', *Psychodynamic Practice,* 28(3): 310–314.

Coltart, N. (2006) The Analysis of an Elderly Patient, 75, (22) in Gabriele Junkers (ed.) *Is It Too Late? Key papers on Psychoanalysis and Aging.* Routledge.

Hoggett, P. (2017) OPUS Lecture, 'Shame in Organizations'.

Krotoski, A. (2025) *The Immortalists- The Death of Death and the Race for Eternal Life.* Bodley Head.

Marris, P. (1993) *Loss and Change.* London: Routledge.

Strassman, B.I. and Garrand, W.A. (2011) 'Alternatives to the Grandmother's Hypothesis', *Human Nature,* 22: 201–222.

Winnicott, D.W. (1969) 'Adolescent process and the Need for Personal confrontation', *Pediatrics,* 44(1).

Index

Note: Page numbers followed by "n" denote endnotes.

For Product Safety Concerns and Information please contact our EU
representative GPSR@taylorandfrancis.com
Taylor & Francis Verlag GmbH, Kaufingerstraße 24, 80331 München, Germany

www.ingramcontent.com/pod-product-compliance
Lightning Source LLC
LaVergne TN
LVHW061723260926
848956LV00030B/264
* 9 7 8 1 0 4 1 0 0 4 9 6 7 *